THE BOY IN BRAZIL

THE BOY IN BRAZIL

LIVING, LOVING AND LEARNING
IN THE LAND OF FOOTBALL

SETH BURKETT

EDITED BY IAN RIDLEY

Floodlit Dreams Ltd
www.floodlitdreams.com

Published by Floodlit Dreams Ltd, 2014.

© Seth Burkett and Floodlit Dreams Ltd, 2014.

A CIP catalogue record for this book is available from the British Library.

ISBN 978-0-99226585-2-6

Floodlit Dreams Ltd
5-6 George St
St Albans
Herts AL3 4ER.

www.floodlitdreams.com

Cover designed by Mike McMonagle
Typeset by Peloton Publishing

CONTENTS

Voce e do tamanho dos seus sonhos...

You are the size of your dreams...

BRAZIL

MANAUS

FORTALEZA

NATAL

RECIFE

MATO GROSSO

Sinop
SORRISO
Lucas do Rio Verde
CUIABA
Cáceres Rondonópolis

Camaçari
Lauro de Freitas
SALVADOR

BRASILIA

BELO HORIZONTE

São Carlos
RIO DE JANEIRO
SÃO PAULO

CURITIBA

PORTO ALEGRE

BRAZIL

SOUTH
AMERICA

0   250   500   750   1000
SCALE IN MILES

1
STAMFORD, TWINNED WITH SÃO PAULO

Anderson Da Silva was a kind man. He was slight with a baby face, glasses and long curly hair, which gave him an endearing and friendly appearance and made him highly approachable. My Dad didn't think he looked old enough to be out of school, though admitted that yes, he was a very nice guy.

He began to appear at games in my second year of playing for the Stamford Under-18 side, sitting just behind my Dad, Dad's mate Dave and Dave's dog. To a young lad who had been besotted with Brazilian football since the age of eight, had burst into tears at their defeat by France in the World Cup final of 1998, such a man was an exotic, intriguing presence here in Lincolnshire, deep in middle England.

Gradually Anderson's story unfolded. He had once been a promising player with São Paulo FC, one of the biggest clubs in Brazil. He was released as a youngster, and although he continued to play, his focus shifted onto helping others realise their dreams. He came over to England in his early 20s to improve his English and chase the money that was on offer from football in Europe.

He had come to Stamford because he had a friend studying English there and played a friendly game for them against a team called Harrowby, who then asked him to turn out for them. Based in a pretty rough area of Grantham, they played in the United Counties League and the style of play was, shall we say, basic. Two years was enough for Anderson. He decided to become an agent, to get Brazilian players to England. For kids from South America, England, with its Premier League, was the promised land.

His first few years were hard. He struggled to speak the language, and had to rely on menial jobs to fund his stay. He was sacked from his first job – tending a nightclub bar – after just a few weeks, when the customers kept on getting the wrong drinks and the management realised that he didn't have a clue what they were saying. Slowly, he settled in; his command of the language improved, his contact list grew.

And his luck turned. He took on a client by the name of Denilson Pereira Neves, whom Arsenal wanted for their midfield. Anderson duly did the deal for Denilson and made his name and a bit of money. Now he could be more selective where he worked. He waited tables at the local branch of the restaurant chain ASK when he felt like it, but he didn't really need the money. His job as an agent was taking up more and more of his time, and he was weighing up whether to devote all of his time to the profession.

I didn't know it then, but he was to play quite a role in my own footballing journey. Me and Denilson having something in common, eh? We would, though, be going in opposite directions.

I love football. Always have. The sport has impacted my life beyond measure, and the experiences that I have had through it have been irreplaceable. It has taken me to the most remote corners of the world, allowed me to befriend all sorts of characters, and, most importantly, given me thousands of hours of enjoyment.

My mother Clare, a primary school supply teacher, reckons I was getting ready for my career as soon I was conceived. She certainly knew I was on my way as I was pretty active in the womb, so perhaps it isn't surprising that the first thing that was put in my cot was a football. Dad, who goes by his middle name of St John and was a head teacher of a primary school, is a bit of a fanatic.

My ball accompanied me throughout childhood growing up in the village of Barnack, just outside Stamford. When I was eventually stopped from playing in the garden because Mum's flowers were getting in the way of the ball, as did a few of her vases, I headed across the road to the Barnack school field with my football tucked under my arm. All of the boys were bigger and older than me, meaning that I had to fetch the ball whenever it went off the pitch or into one of the many gardens surrounding the field, regardless of whether I was put in goal (as the youngest I often was) or not.

Football 'up the school' was my life outside of learning the seven times table. When not at school my best friend Jamie would call my house phone every morning at nine and ask Mum if Seth was in. Once I was put on the line, Jamie would always ask if I 'fancied football up the school'. Of course I did. We would play from 9.30am till 1pm, when we would go back to one of our houses to eat lunch and play football games on the PlayStation. At two we would resurface, playing for another four hours before our families could have us back for dinner. My life was perfect, and it only got better when Jamie began to invite his neighbour Callum up the school. Callum was a year younger than me, and smaller than everyone else, automatically making him goalkeeper and chief ball boy.

The extra practice I got now Callum had relieved me of my goalkeeping duties brought on an improvement to my game which led to me signing for the Peterborough United academy team as an eight-year-old. It was a great honour for me and was serious stuff.

We were given homework to do – 30 minutes of keepieuppies, skills and skipping – each night and following matches we had to write a personal report of our game. There would be nutrition talks and regular feedback regarding our performance. At the age of nine, I was introduced to futsal – short for *futebol de salao*, a form of indoor football that helped skills and technique and which would come to play a significant part in my life. I loved it all, loved the seriousness of my passion and representing a team I by now supported with such gusto.

My Dad had taken me two years earlier to watch my first Peterborough game. I formed an immediate attachment, crying in my seat and accusing Bournemouth of cheating after Peterborough conceded a 95th minute equaliser in one of the first games I attended, only leaving once the stadium had fully emptied. When Peterborough hadn't won, my Mum knew to steer well clear of Dad until the next day. Although she didn't have much of an opinion on football, she knew how it could affect those that did.

Dad had always encouraged my football interests, but he appeared to be the only member of my family who was passionate about the game. Both of his parents were tennis fans with a general lack of interest in football. My Mum's side of the family were similarly untouched by 'The Beautiful Game'. When my Grandpa agreed to play football with me he used to stand in goal and kick the ball as far away as possible, watching my boundless energy as I raced to retrieve the ball with a fear that once again in the near future he would be forced to attempt to save a shot.

As far as my living family, then, it was just Dad and I who liked the game. Despite this, I was assured that there had been some distant relatives, now dead, who had a similar passion for football. The most talented of these, my great great uncle Charlie Williams, had played in goal for Arsenal in the early 1900s according to my grandparents, and that would stand up when we later came to look into it. He had also lived in Brazil, they reckoned, which sounded rather more fanciful.

As a kid who was becoming captivated by Brazilian football, the very thought fired my imagination, though. It was as if there was something in my genes that drew me to the country and gave me a passion not just for football but an appreciation of all things Brazilian.

The 1998 World Cup in France was one of my first experiences of a major football event, and my youthful eagerness turned itself into support for the nation with the happy fans, the smiling players and the phenomenon, Ronaldo, playing up front. Most of all though, I liked Brazil's kit. Those bright yellow shirts tinged with green were complemented by blue shorts and white socks that drew together all the colours of the country's flag and evoked the happiness and exotic style with which the team who wore them played.

In the stands a sea of yellow swayed up and down, left and right, as the games went on. The supporters, comprising all ages, races and both sexes, bounded about in their backing, expressing their devotion through their movements, their dances and their singing in a loud, cheerful display.

Brazil's defeat to the host nation in the final only endeared them further to me. The scenes of sorrow in the crowd and the tears shed by the distraught players on the pitch were reactions to such a terrible event that I could relate to. The emotion showed the sheer human passion running through Brazilians.

Roberto Carlos was my favourite player. He was left footed just like me, had massive legs and a powerful shot. His speciality was a swerving bullet of a free kick, often hit from distances of around 40 yards. At nights I'd go into my garden and pretend to be him, kicking the ball as hard as I could towards the makeshift goals my Dad had built. If it went in, Brazil were World Champions and if it didn't, I'd take another two shots.

Unfortunately, I wasn't playing like a Brazilian on the pitch. After two years at Peterborough United I was released. I was mortified. I cried and cried and cried. It felt like my life had ended. That feeling passed when I was taken on by Northampton Town and I had high hopes again during four years there. More disappointment came at the age of 14 with another release. It started to dawn on me that the dream of professional football was not looking likely to become a reality.

Once again I wept, but the tears did not last as long. Following a few unsuccessful trials with other professional clubs – Leicester City, Boston United and another spell at Peterborough that would not result in any offer to become a pro – reality bit and I gave up my focus on becoming a footballer. At the age of 16, I decided instead to concentrate on academia and gaining a place at a good university. Just out of a desire to keep playing, though, I joined my local team, Stamford AFC, who played in Division One South of the Unibond League, the Northern Premier.

Dad still supported my football career as much as ever, and continued to watch every game I played, both home and away. He was pretty happy he no longer had to do the 80-minute drive to Northampton four times a week and assured me that Stamford wasn't such a bad option for a football career anyway. Sure, the quaint little market town was too middle-class to be a footballing hotbed, but at least this way I could go to university and get a good job whilst playing football on the side. The first team at Stamford paid a bit of money, and Dad said this could be my 'luxuries' money on top of a basic wage from whatever job I decided to do.

It sounded all right to me, and I was by now realistic about life and football, but that was what my head said. In my heart, I had that feeling that I should have been playing for Peterborough. I still yearned, still wished they had never released me.

Mum didn't come to watch me so much. I had a nasty habit of breaking bones when she turned up on the touchline and she got scared of me playing with the big boys. On the rare occasions she worked up enough courage to attend a match, she'd more often than not embarrass me.

One particular episode came when I had just broken into the first team at Stamford as a scrawny 16-year-old. Mum accompanied Dad to my third game in the squad, when I was sent on as a second half substitute against promotion-chasing Glapwell. Almost my first action in the game was to stick my head into a 50/50 challenge. My opponent decided to use his foot, and proceeded to miss the ball and connect his metal studs with my head. I'm not sure if it hurt or not. I had blacked out by the time I hit the floor. I wasn't out for long, but a familiar voice greeted my reawakening to the world.

'Sethy boy! My Sethy boy! Is he OK?!'

Mum had jumped from her seat in the main stand and sprinted round to the opposite side of the pitch where the collision had taken place. Now she was standing amongst the handful of fans who fancied themselves as football hooligans in the terrace.

'Becky! Becky!' Mum was frantically screaming at the physio, looking like she was on the verge of tears. Becky slowly led me to the side of the pitch. Everything was blurred. Mum put her arm on my shoulder. I could hear the wannabe hooligans giggling.

'Ooooh, Sethy boy. Are you okay Sethy boy?' came the mocking high-pitched cries. I never lived that one down. Football can be a cruel place.

Dad decided to make my sister Kezia, who was 18 months younger than me, accompany him to the next match instead. She had been quite resistant at first, but Dad assured her that if she came, he would make me go to watch one of her ballet shows. After much persuasion Kizzie came. She wasn't much company for Dad. She spent the whole game either looking at her phone and listening to her iPod or moaning. It was too cold. At least when I watched her prance about on stage it was warm. And why was it so boring?

Dad tried a similarly unsuccessful experiment with my Gran the next game. This was the local derby against our fierce rivals Grantham, and I had done well enough to gain a starting place in the team. A large crowd gathered at Grantham's blustery stadium to see us fall to a 4-0 deficit at half time. We walked off the pitch to loud boos. A number of fans had grouped around the tunnel to let their views be known to the 11 useless Stamford men in red. And right in the middle of that group was my beaming Gran.

'Seth! Seth!' she yelled. 'Over here, I'm here. You're doing really well!', she was shouting. And waving at me with the biggest of grins on her face. Gran never did get the hang of football.

We lost the game 4-1 and Gran came into the changing room after the game to tell me to hurry up as she was hungry. I don't know how she got past the stewards. Our manager was still doing his post-match team talk, and was in the middle of an elaborate and passionate outburst of expletives just when she interrupted. Gran was ushered back upstairs to the clubhouse by Melly the kit man, who assured her that he'd hurry me up once our manager was done.

Up in the clubhouse, Gran befriended the Stamford chairman and asked him if I was the best player in the team. She thought I was, but after I'd hurried up and joined her she relayed the information back that I needed to get bigger and stronger. And then she introduced me to her new friend the chairman.

Fortunately I wasn't just playing for the first team, and had just about managed to keep my credibility in the Stamford

Under 18 side. Far fewer people watched the Under 18s, and none of them knew me as 'Sethy boy'. After much searching, Dad had finally found someone to watch my games with who wouldn't embarrass me. Every week he and Dave – the owner of my sister's ballet school – would go and sit in some old rickety stand in Northamptonshire with Dave's dog, a Yorkshire terrier who went by the name of Alfie, for company.

At home games, the three of them would be joined by a cluster of parents and loyal Stamford supporters who braved the cold conditions to cheer us on. Along with Anderson Da Silva, who was about to make our team an offer that I for one certainly couldn't refuse.

2
SPOTTED IN SALVADOR

Anderson's proposition was that in return for £500, he could organise a 16-day football tour for us at the end of the season. To Brazil. I for one needed no second bidding and dashed home to tell Mum and Dad and beg them for some financial help. They readily agreed, thankfully, with the proviso that I also had to help myself. So, after some fund-raising stunts, which included packing bags in Morrisons, shortly after my A levels I found myself jetting off to the North East of Brazil, to the state of Bahia.

We were mobbed by photographers and camera crews as soon as we entered the airport terminal at the city of Salvador. We couldn't believe how much importance we were given by the Brazilian media. Most of us were excited enough about having our match report put in the local newspaper each week – and I was happy just to see my name in the list of unused substitutes for the first team – so suddenly to be giving interviews for large terrestrial channels was a bit bizarre but wonderful. We felt like we were in the Premier League, like we were stars. We collected our luggage buoyed, already sensing that this was a special country.

The first night was a real culture shock. After a dinner of plain rice and tasteless beans in a crumbling hotel we were led across floor of broken glass in a graffiti-covered courtyard to our rooms. These were horrible – small, poorly laid out and lacking not only glass in the window (which probably explained the thousands of broken pieces in the courtyard), but also air conditioning.

The air was hot and humid, like being in a sauna, and there was no real solution to the problem – open the windows and let all the bugs and insects in or keep them closed and bake. To make matters worse for me personally, my bed was next to the toilet. To exit the room I had to jump over the toilet, which was located between my bed and the next. Disgusted, we headed to Anderson's room to complain. We found him asleep in his bed, his passport and mobile phone clutched close to his body in a firm grasp. What had we let ourselves in for?

It would be one of the most nervous night's sleeps I had ever had. We were all well aware that there was nothing stopping any potential burglars from hopping through the window and stealing our stuff, and we had all heard the horror stories about crime in Brazil.

Thankfully things soon improved. For all of his positives, Anderson had what I would come to discover were widespread cavalier Brazilian attitudes towards organisation and time. Only after that terrible night's sleep did he reveal that our first game of the tournament was that evening against Brazil Under 17s. Now the reasons why we were mobbed by the media became apparent. Now we realised why the trip was costing only £500 each – and not just because of the state of the accommodation. The Brazilians were so thrilled at us coming out there that they had heavily subsidised our stay.

The fact that we would be facing the Brazilian national team was a real shock to a team more used to taking on the finest from Eynesbury Rovers and Irchester United. We had expected tough games in Brazil, but to play against the national team?

Sadly, I and five of my team-mates had to watch the game from the bench situated in front of the one stand that ran the length of the touchline at the stadium in the Bahia town of

Camacari, 50 kilometres from Salvador. We had found out before we left for the tournament that we would be too old for it. Anderson said he'd fully understand if we no longer wanted to come along but of course we did – how many other opportunities would we get to have a taste of Brazilian football? Anyway, we could still play in any friendly games that were organised.

And so we were helpless as our raw team was pulled apart by a tricky winger called Philippe Coutinho, who we all admitted looked to have a bright future. Coutinho bagged a hat-trick in front of a crowd of 8,000 as Brazil triumphed 8-0 and Anderson later told us that he was destined for big things, that Inter Milan had offered a lot of money and he would join them on his 18th birthday. Later he would end up at Liverpool. We had been right about that bright future. At least our manager's son, Jake, could tell the story of how he once got sent off for bringing down an £8.5 million-rated player.

Despite our clear lack of ability, we were surrounded by excited youngsters who all demanded our autographs and although I hadn't actually played, I had caught the Brazilian bug. The way they played the game was a joy. They were so fluid, their game focused on individual creativity and brilliance. The crowd was fantastic, so hostile but supportive of the home team. I couldn't wait to experience it for myself. The mood was similarly positive as we walked to the bus – to avoid conceding double figures against such a great team, wow, what an achievement! We were soon brought back down to Earth as we boarded the bus, however, when confronted by masses of hyperactive youngsters. 'Eight! Eight!' they screamed, holding up eight fingers and laughing.

Anderson was well aware that the six over-aged boys were itching to kick a ball about. As an agent he had strong links with numerous clubs in Brazil and he used them to arrange for us to train with the under 18 side of Esporte Clube Vitoria, who played in the top division of Brazilian football. We were to report to Vitoria for one session each day of the week.

Their training complex was built into the hillside at the top of a long, winding road. Salvador was a beautiful city, of bright colours, exotic wildlife and beaches of white sand stretching for miles but this was our introduction to the contradiction of Brazil. In this city of more than 2.5 million people, shacks littered the sides of the hill, placed wherever the owner could find a space. It was a million miles from our privileged ways of life in England.

The first thing we saw was a dirt pitch which had around it boards of cartoon drawings depicting Vitoria's lion mascot playing football. This pitch was left open for anyone to play on. In each drawing the lion had a large smile. Past this there was a barrier with an armed guard, who nodded to let us through to the changing rooms. Next to the changing rooms was the player accommodation, used for the youth teams to stay during the season. They were basic concrete structures with bunk beds. The windows were barred. Prison cells in England looked nicer – from pictures of them I had seen, that was.

The training pitches were all down the hill, past a large, stunning EC Vitoria badge designed by a gardener out of shrubs, on a large area of flat land. There, to the right, was Vitoria's stadium, its capacity 36,000. There were two training pitches for the first team and two for all of the junior teams to fight over. The first team pitches were in pristine condition, unlike those for the juniors, used all day every day. Not even the best groundsman could have done anything about them.

Vitoria certainly had that area of employment covered. Even though they must have had the financial muscle to buy top-of-the-range mowers and employ the best in the business, they seemed to understand that they were representing the community, most of whom suffered from desperate poverty. And so they hired 20 people from the shacks, giving them a large hat, scissors and a stool.

These 20 people then split between two of the four pitches, sitting on their stools with their large hats covering them from the glaring sun, and cut the grass with scissors. When they had finished a patch they moved their stools onto the next area. When they all finished this process they would move on to the next pitch, and by the time they finished that it was time to start all over again. It was menial work, but it allowed the people valid employment and enough money to take home for food.

I loved the training. Everything was done with the ball. The first half of each session would often be conducted with a tiny ball – usually a size one. With this ball we would do keepy-uppies and then dribbling activities. Big toe, little toe, big toe, little toe. The coaches made us run up and down dribbling like this, alternating between both feet. Then we would play a game. After our third session Anderson approached me.

'The manager likes you,' he said. 'His left back has been called up by Brazil under 20s and he needs someone to fill the slot. They have a friendly game tomorrow. Can you do the job?' Can I do the job? I was ready to leap out of my skin. I was trying to sound cool when I replied, 'Yes, sure,' but I snatched the opportunity as quickly as I could.

I knew that rest was vital, and that evening I went to bed early in our newly upgraded hotel. Or at least I tried to. My team-mates had no need to go to bed early, and were evidently quite bored without me. Little more than 30 minutes after I turned my light off there was an almighty commotion, and suddenly they were all there in my room. Three of them held me down whilst the rest whipped out canisters of shaving foam. Someone was kind enough to remove my underwear during the whole ordeal, despite my valiant efforts to kick them. There was shaving foam everywhere. I was writhing about, screaming for them to stop. Then I managed to break free. I spotted my underwear in somebody's hands and went after the culprit. He was quicker than I expected, and I ended up chasing him all the way to the beach before he took pity and gave my boxers back.

I got only five hours of sleep before my big day and awoke slightly tired and sticky but buzzing. The match was scheduled for midday, a real test when the sun was at its strongest, especially when the Brazilian interpretation of my left back position suggested that I spend the whole game running up and down the pitch.

Indeed, I had a distinct feeling throughout the 90 minutes that I was just seconds from dropping down dead. It was horrible. Breathing was incredibly hard and it felt like I was playing in a sauna. Within 20 minutes I wanted the full-time whistle. Somehow I managed to last the whole game and the coach seemed happy enough with a 2-0 victory.

Fortunately for me, Anderson had been watching the whole game with a friend named Emerson Mattheus he had brought in to help us out at the tournament. It turned out that Emerson had been impressed enough by my performance to enquire as to my availability for the next season, starting in January 2010. He was due to take charge of an under 18 team in the small city of Sorriso in central Brazil and he wondered if I fancied playing for his team.

Sorriso, he said, had been entered for the Copa São Paulo, a prestigious youth competition which takes place in early January each year, with 104 teams entering. Sorriso were the champions of their state, Mato Grosso, but in need of reinforcements for such a high quality tournament. They would need me out there in the autumn to prepare.

It was an amazing offer and I rang my parents quickly to tell them. They would back me if I wanted to accept. But there was university, there was uprooting myself... I had a lot of thinking to do over our remaining days in Brazil.

Our tournament games were dotted over the state of Bahia of which Salvador is the capital, in Camacari and Lauro de Frei-tas. We were beaten 2-0 by Salvador and 5-2 by Lauro. We then learned that Anderson had scheduled several friendly games which had no age requirements. Our first game was against Vitoria, and with our reinforcements we were a much more competitive team, eventually succumbing to a creditable 4-1 defeat. We finally enjoyed a win, by 3-0 over a team of Bahia triallists, a match watched by a player who would go on to star for Barcelona. Neymar was training with Santos on the next pitch ahead of a match with Vitoria.

Then came our final game, another illustration of Brazilian ways, scheduled for a midday kick-off against the full youth team of Emerson's former club, Bahia, the other big Salvador team. Our bus was due to leave the hotel at 10am for a midday kick-off. By midday it still hadn't arrived. We eventually man-aged to get to Bahia's training complex for 1pm. but the train-ing ground was empty. After a long search Anderson managed to hunt down a caretaker, who informed him that the coaches felt like playing the game at 4pm instead. The whole episode simply emphasised the laid-back atmosphere.

Once again we competed but lost 3-0. My appetite had been suitably whetted, though. I had acclimatised enough and no longer felt like I was about to suffer from a minor heart attack any time I broke into a jog. The style of play suited my lack of physicality and the genuine passion exhibited by the Brazilians struck a chord in my heart.

In truth, Emerson's offer didn't take much thinking about. I had wanted to go to Loughborough University to do Sports Science but they offered me Sports Science with English, which

I was not keen on, so I was going to take a year out to reapply anyway. (I had also applied for Cambridge but I don't think they were too impressed at being my second choice). And I had always wanted to play football abroad. It felt right, though it would not be for everyone, I guess.

I got on well with my team-mates and talked it through particularly with my room-mate, Tom Stuffins. He didn't know how he would manage coming back out to Brazil. Like a lot of the lads, he got homesick and struggled to adapt to the food and the notable drop in standard of living. When he saw the player accommodation at Vitoria, he thought I would be crazy but he wished me all the best and urged me to take the opportunity anyway. I think that's how a lot of the lads saw it. They were pleased for me but not really envious.

Soon after getting home, I learned I had three As and two Bs in English, Sports Science, General Studies, Geography and Biology but university could wait. Mum and Dad were insistent I should go for the Brazil opportunity. They had always been supportive and told me I should follow my dreams. And so, excited, I followed my dreams.

3
SEFI OF SORRISO

The journey from Stamford to Sorriso took 32 hours and was full of apprehension and complication, though the hardest part was saying my goodbyes. First of all there were my three best friends Bilf, Josh and Marco, who had sombrely come into my room in Barnack to wish me good luck. Bilf reminded me how I hadn't even been good enough to play for Peterborough – who everyone knew were rubbish – so what chance did I have in Brazil? Marco told me the story of his dad's friend who had his Achilles tendon slashed by a mugger in Rio de Janeiro while he was taking a photo of the sunset. It must have been the thirtieth time I'd heard it. Josh just said he'd miss me. We all hugged. Mum took a picture.

Then it was off down to Heathrow Airport. Dad was swelling with pride as I left them to go through security. Mum broke into uncontrollable tears. Kizzie gave me a hug. When I turned around, they were gone. I didn't know when I'd next see them. It was a horrible feeling.

It was actually happening. It was now mid-November, four months after I had come back from the Brazilian tour, and for much of that time it had looked as if it would not come off, given the trouble involved in sorting out documents. All the homework I had been doing on Sorriso, the place and football club, seemed at times as if it might have been in vain.

The city did not exist until 1985, I discovered. Created out of cleared rainforest in central Brazil, it soon attracted numerous people who were not only enticed by the cheap land on offer, but also the cheerful city name. 'Sorriso' translated as 'smile', though the name selection was not intentional. In fact, it was a reference to the Italian immigrants who only cultivated rice in the area. 'So riso' means 'only rice' but the words ended up being merged to form the final name of the city.

The terrain of the area was exceptional for cultivating crops, some of the flattest and most fertile land in Brazil. Over the years, it had specialised in the production of soybean, and developed to become the national capital of agribusiness. It was now the biggest producer of soybean in the World, which is how many of the 70,000 Sorriso residents came to make their riches.

Deep in the heart of Brazil, and South America, Sorriso was some 1,500 miles from Rio and the same from Manaus in the Amazon forest to the North (where England, it would turn out, would play Italy in their opening game of the 2014 World Cup finals). Whereas Salvador was located next to beautiful long, golden beaches, Sorriso could not have been further from the coast. Indeed, it would take a two-day car drive to get to the nearest beach.

The club, Sorriso Esporte Clube, had both a youth team and a full-time professional senior team, their Mato Grosso state leagues running parallel from late January to April. From May to December, the national leagues took place but featured only the top ranked 100 clubs, the top 20 clubs comprising such giants as as Flamengo and Fluminense from Rio and Corinthians and Palmeiras from São Paulo forming Serie A.

That meant another 700 professional clubs in the country left with no fixtures between May and December, so states often organised their own cups for part of this time. The Mato Grosso cup took place from late August to November. SEC were ranked 264th in the country by the *Confederacao Brasileira de*

Futebol – the Brazilian equivalent of the Football Association. In status, it was probably around the same level as the Conference in England.

Finally I was getting on a plane to see and experience all this for myself. I flew via Lisbon to Brasilia, where I felt lost as I searched the airport – so big, so foreign – for my internal flight to Cuiaba, the nearest airport to Sorriso. This was not ideal considering that, after the Brazilians had taken so long to get us through passport control, I was left with just 45 minutes to catch my connecting flight.

It suddenly occurred to me that I had never been in an airport on my own before, let alone in a foreign country on the other side of the World. I suddenly felt my youthfulness, how exposed I was to anyone who could quite easily take advantage of me.

My fearful expression must have been evident as I was approached by a Swedish man. He was a gymnastics coach, and was in Brazil to improve his own coaching knowledge, having previously worked with the United States gymnastics team. He had been to Brazil regularly and was comfortable in the airport. He kindly pushed me in the direction of the line for my connecting flight. In another kind twist of fate, the queue wasn't too long, just tediously slow moving.

After a frustrating wait I made it to the front where I was brusquely informed that I was in the wrong queue. The airport attendant directed me to the actual queue I needed to be in. I was sweating quite heavily now, my heart bouncing around my chest. I had 15 minutes left until take-off. Terrible thoughts flooded my head – what if I missed the flight? I'd lose my contract with Sorriso. I'd be stuck in Brazil, unable to afford a flight home. What was that film? Oh yes, *The Terminal*.

I needn't have worried. I was in Brazil after all. I reached the gate with two minutes to spare after being fast-tracked through the correct queue. The flight took off half-an-hour late, which I was coming to learn was actually pretty good when it came to Brazilian timing. It was only when I was in the air that I realised I had no clue who was picking me up or how I was actually getting to Sorriso.

The question, whilst troubling, was not as disturbing as the flight. I'd never been in an aeroplane that vibrated so much. It was like we were going through permanent turbulence. Overwhelming relief flooded through me when the wheels touched down in Cuiaba. I stepped out of the potential death-trap into torrential rain, a lovely feeling in the oppressive heat.

The airport building was a lot less intimidating than the one in Brasilia. It was tiny, more like a reception area in a hotel. There was just one carousel, and my suitcase was the first to appear. Optimistic, I collected it and headed to where I hoped Emerson would meet me. A man approached me.

'Michel?'

'No, Seth', I replied.

'No, no, Michel'.

'You, Sorriso?' I asked, desperately trying hand gestures. He nodded, before telling me in broken English that he was picking up a Michel from Portugal. I think that was what he meant anyway.

'No. Me. Seth. Sorriso. Play *futebol*.' I was getting frantic. This appeared to be the man who was supposed to be taking me. It was just a shame that he wasn't aware of it. He excused himself and embarked on a long, long phone call. My heart was doing somersaults. After about 20 minutes he nodded to tell me that I could jump in with him. We just had to wait for Michel.

Finally, a muscular teenager around six feet tall stepped into the airport reception. What was most striking about him was not his black curly hair, but more his choice of attire. Michel was obviously proud of his body, and had made a conscious effort to emphasise his bulging arms by donning a bright pink vest, together with tight jeans and running trainers.

Undeterred by his episode with me, the man approached Michel with a forceful, outstretched hand and a smile. This was definitely the boy he was supposed to be picking up. He motioned for both of us to follow him into a small, white 1980s Fiat Punto. I still wasn't sure that this was who was supposed to be picking me up, but I was too tired to care and grateful to have some company.

I sat in the back and attempted to make sense of the conversation that the man and Michel were having. It appeared that he was the Chairman of Sorriso and had invested a great deal of money into the club. He really should have put a bit of money aside to invest in his car, whose age was no secret thanks to the excessive rust.

The Chairman seemed a self-important man. He talked loudly and took little notice of what Michel was saying. He was on the phone for most of the journey. I had decided to sit behind Michel. Although the Chairman had seemingly played football in the past – he claimed to have played for Corinthians, though I was sceptical – he had developed a pot belly which was out of proportion to the rest of his body. His car seat was tilted quite far back, giving his stomach just enough room to fit under the steering wheel. I guessed him to be around 40 years old but had no Portuguese to ask him any questions.

As a break from the self-importance, the man stopped the car and paid for a buffet for the three of us. It was here that I was able to talk to Michel, who I discovered was a goalkeeper, one of Anderson's players, and who had previously played in Brazil for Emerson. Michel had a friendly, gentle demeanour and was softly spoken.

Feeling well-fed and watered, I dropped into a deep sleep back in the Punto, which was frequently slowed by bouts of astonishingly heavy showers. We even had to come to a halt a couple of times to wait for the apocalyptic rain to relent. Anderson had told me that the journey would take 'a few' hours. I believed him – Sorriso is in the same state as Cuiaba after all. I had neglected to take into account that Mato Grosso, like many of the other Brazilian states, covered a vast area. In fact, in area the state is four times bigger than the United Kingdom.

After eight hours of driving on dusty, pot-holed roads, with views of nothing more than expansive fields of crops, punctuated by a settlement every now and again, we came to a small city. We drove through a dusty favela at the edge of an industrial estate, filled with box houses created from whatever materials the owners could find. On the edge of the favela we stopped at what appeared to be a garage, I presumed to fill up with petrol. It turned out that 'Casa dos Filtros' – literally 'House of Filters' and indeed a former garage - was my new home.

The Chairman gestured for us to get our suitcases and follow him and tentatively I obeyed. Casa dos Filtros had a big up-and-over front door and a corrugated iron roof. The door led into a large communal area and kitchen. There was a long bench running from one wall to the other, and a television opposite this. I wondered why there was a toilet brush on the table. The house was empty. It was late afternoon and the team was presumably training.

We were taken to a room on the left, where the Chairman told us to leave our suitcases. The room was a little bigger than my one at home - but this one I had to share with five Brazilians (or four and Michel). Three bunk beds were shoved around the perimeter of the room, leaving an area of about four square metres in the middle. The windows had bars covering them, though one of the windows had a bar missing.

The most notable object in the room was the large air conditioning box in the top corner of the room, which had been turned up to full in the absence of the residents. It felt like a refrigerator in there. Quotes, printed on paper in large font, were pinned to the walls of the room and I wished that I knew what they meant. A couple were clearly marked as being Biblical and I suspected the others were motivational.

The concrete bathroom was a collection of shared, open showers, three toilets with no doors and a urinal under a washing line. Shower curtains hung limply where the toilet doors should have been in a vain attempt to preserve the user's dignity, though one toilet lacked a curtain and was utterly exposed. This same toilet was missing a toilet brush, and I couldn't help but think the brush on the dining room table was in the wrong place.

And was that brush needed in that toilet. Flies were hovering around what the last user had deposited on the seat and the other two toilets had urine covering the floor. Deciding that this was the lesser of two evils I carefully tiptoed in to relieve myself. It seemed my personal hygiene was rapidly about to go downhill. We got back into the Chairman's car and headed across town.

The beautiful scenery that was so overwhelming in Salvador was absent from the Sorriso area. Instead there were miles and miles of plain, boring soybean fields, stretching as far as the eye could see. There remained uncleared patches of rainforest around the outskirts of the city and not until you got 10 minutes out of the place was there much more foliage, replete with tropical birds of all colours of the rainbow.

The city of Sorriso itself, however, was rather plain. Nice, but not exactly inspiring. Like many of the newly built areas, such as the notoriously bland Brasilia, it was a bit too manufactured, almost perfectly square. At the centre were two parks, filled with ice-cream vendors, cafes/diners known locally as luncheonettes and benches, along with the newly built shopping centre, cinema and television studios complex, providing the social hub of the city. When the football stadium and churches weren't open of course.

The Chairman parked his car at the Estadio Egidio Jose Preima, home of Sorriso Esporte Clube, and we walked through the entrance to see our new team being put through their paces by Emerson.

The stadium had been built on the edge of the city, and it looked out on to gentle rolling hills punctuated by the odd house. There was only one large concrete, terraced stand, with no seats as such, that ran the length of one side of the ground and which I was told could accommodate around 5,000 people. A roof spanned across thirty metres at its centre but the rest of the ground was open. From the stand, the handful of supporters watching the training session could see the impressive view. The substitute benches were opposite the stand, but the changing rooms were hidden by the hill.

We entered the ground at the centre of the stand, coming out at the halfway line. A commentary box sat above the walkway, with the message '*Obrigado por prestigar o esporte*' – thank you for honouring the sport – painted across it. A large wired fence, combined with a running track, separated the stand from the pitch. I could just imagine the fans jumping on this fence, going crazy as I scored yet another match winner for their beloved team.

Closer inspection of the pitch put my daydream in jeopardy, I wasn't sure how I was going to be able to play on it. There was a distinct lack of grass. Where there was grass it was knee high, wispy rather than thick but knee high nevertheless. There were dusty patches of earth dotted all around. The only areas that had grass at an acceptable height were the penalty areas.

There were 31 players training and I would find out they were all ages from 13 to 18. That was the way here, it seemed; if they were good enough and strong enough, they could compete with players more senior. Emerson had them playing a match, and he bounced over to me and Michel, who would take the squad up to 33, of whom 28 would end up going to the Copa São Paolo.

'Ah, Sefi!' he said, approaching me first, firmly shaking my hand with a broad beam across his face, showing his pearl white teeth. I noted the England cap he was wearing, presumably for my benefit. Emerson cut a porcine figure, stocky if not fat. His calf muscles were not far off the girth of my torso.

Emerson had been a good player, also a left back, and had played at a high standard, with Bahia of Salvador in the 1980s. Lots of people recognised him and he enjoyed the fame. He had even been capped by Brazil at Under 23 level, and had accumulated enough money from his long spell in the Brazilian top flight to drive around in the biggest, shiniest, whitest Range Rover I'd ever seen. The healthy tan that he sported blended in perfectly with his bleached blonde hair, taking the attention away from his snout-like nose. His smile was infectious, his voice booming and his personality endearing. I immediately felt welcome.

Back in Casa dos Filtros my team-mates stared at me inquisitively. They had never met an English boy before. They introduced themselves before dinner, but were unsure of how to build conversation. I had learned a few words in Salvador, and I tested one out to try and befriend them.

'*Pinto*,' I said – a slang word for penis – and they roared approving laughs. Suddenly they were jabbering at me from all angles, encouraging me to say more rude words in Portuguese. I acted the parrot, copying all that I heard to the delight of my onlookers.

Lucas, who I would find out was a defender, was especially vocal in encouraging me to say phrases. Although he was of slight build, he had a mean face. At some stage in his life he had decided that his curly hair gave off the wrong impression, of being soft, and he had covered his arms with tattoos to try and alter the perception. Despite this he couldn't have been more hospitable, and he really eased my transition into the house. Unfortunately he couldn't get a grasp of my name.

'Jeff?' he wondered...'Jeffy? Sefi?' Sefi would do, at least that had an S in it. I had encountered this problem in Salvador. It seemed that Brazilians just couldn't pronounce my name.

After my little show, the Chairman arrived and encouraged me to go along to a local game with some of my team-mates. Andrei was Sorriso's star striker, and was one of the few players who actually lived in the city. On top of this he could speak a little English. Chandler and Viniscius – the team's central defenders and two of my new room-mates – joined us.

Viniscius had the same sort of porky attributes as Emerson and also had a little pig tail growing out of the back of his head to complete the illusion. He appeared loud and confident. Chandler was taller, quieter and quite obviously very fashion conscious, perhaps more so than Viniscius. Rumour had it that he had served a prison sentence, though nobody knew for what. Perhaps Viniscius put the rumour round himself to frighten us, or me at least.

Andrei drove us to the stadium I had been at just a few hours before, and I took my seat alongside a few hundred other spectators. I quickly learned I was at a game where the teams were competing to be the best amateur team in Sorriso. Andrei pointed out the No. 8 for the team in blue and white. 'Watch him... He very good.'

Apparently the No. 8 had had trials with Portsmouth but I didn't really get the chance to assess his performance as quite quickly he managed to get himself sent off for what the referee deemed an unacceptable shoulder barge. The No. 8

subsequently deemed it unacceptable that the referee should send him off for such an innocuous tickle of his opponent's shoulder, and reacted by pushing the referee several times. The referee eventually fell to the ground, sparking havoc. Both teams piled in, with punches being thrown everywhere. In the corner of my eye I made out the linesman from the far touchline. He was hitting one of the players with his flag. Someone tried to stop him and he turned around and jabbed them in the midriff with his flag. The referee, now back on his feet, was helplessly tooting his whistle. Nobody was listening.

Somehow the madness fizzled out, and the No. 8 was ejected from the pitch. The game re-started only to stop a matter of minutes later. The No. 8 had re-emerged with a beer in his hand, still wearing his match shorts but nothing else. Carrying his beer in one hand, his boot bag in the other, he embarked on an infuriatingly slow walk across the pitch and prevented any play for another two minutes.

Welcome, Sefi Burkett (they would later have some fun with my surname too), to the wonderful world of Brazilian football.

4
MEDIA DARLING

I returned home late ready for bed. My team-mates were still awake, eager to make me say more rude words. I obliged them for a couple of minutes before heading to my room. Some followed, continuing to talk to me as I stripped off and got into the top layer of the bunk beds I shared with Pelezinho, a midfield player. Great name. We had two people nicknamed Pele in our team. The one at the lower level of my bunk bed was the smaller one so the suffix 'zinho' had been added to his name to enable us to differentiate between the two. This is common practice for Brazilians – 'inho' is put at the end of those of who are smaller, 'ao' at the end of those bigger .

I really hoped there was another Sefi in the team, as I dreamed of running out to make my debut with 'Sefizinho 3' proudly displayed on the back of my fresh Sorriso shirt. With this pleasant thought in my mind I turned my back on the few Brazilians left trying to keep me talking with them and closed my eyes.

I was dropping off when I turned back over and could just make out a figure. I opened my eyes to find someone staring at me with a loving look in his eye. He noticed my eyes flickering and his mouth curved into a smile, his eyes, just visible under his long floppy hair, still fixed on me.

I recognised the boy, whose name was Fernando. I was pretty sure that he had been training alongside me at Vitoria, but this familiarity did nothing to prevent me from being perturbed by his fixation. The next time I opened my eyes he was gone.

The next thing I knew, my feet were being shaken. It was the kit man, Oswaldo, a man in his mid-20s and one of two backroom staff who lived at Casa dos Filtros, the goalkeeping coach Joaquim being the other. 'Train. *Vamos, vamos,*' Oswaldo insisted. I looked at my phone. It was 7.30am. I couldn't remember the last time I had been up this early.

I wearily followed Oswaldo to a little passage by the bathroom where he reached down into a bucket labelled 'Sefi' and handed me a blue vest full of holes, black shorts with a number 32 and black socks. I changed and followed Chandler into the dining room, where a breakfast of bread rolls and chocolate milk was laid out for us.

Training began at 8.30, and the team bus driver arrived at 8.15 to drive us the short distance to the stadium. Emerson was wearing his England cap again and welcomed me with the same joyful embrace. The session began with Emerson gathering the squad, and talking very quickly in Portuguese for a good 20 minutes. I made out a couple of 'Inglese' and 'Sefi' references, but hadn't a clue what else was being said. Two other coaches backed Emerson up, standing behind him with folded arms to give the impression of security guards. The session itself was quite decent. I was quite awful. I was so bad that in the crossing drill at the end of the session Emerson made me have two touches before crossing the ball into the box. All the Brazilians crossed the ball first time.

Ignoring my shameful display, the Chairman quickly bundled me into the back of his Punto and drove me to the local television station. I was to be a live studio guest on a sports show, aided by a translator.

The TV station was located inside a colourfully decorated and modern shopping centre, which seemed quite out of place compared to the surroundings back at Casa dos Filtros. I

followed the Chairman into Studio 2, where I was warmly greeted by the waiting host. I was on screen for around 20 minutes
and was asked a whole host of questions, about my motivations
for playing in Brazil, my style of play and my English way of
life. Emerson joined us for the last 10 minutes, and he was also
quizzed on me and what I could bring to the team.

Back at Casa dos Filtros my team-mates had seen my
performance. I think that they'd enjoyed my gushing answers declaring the World's love for Brazil and their football,
and they proceeded to give me plenty of feedback: 'You say
errrr much'...'You have big nose'...'You ugly but your sister, she
beautiful'...'Jeff I marry you sister?' I shouldn't have mentioned
my sister. Dudu, a small and agile attacking midfield player, was
particularly assertive that everything to do with England was
'gay', everything that had ever come out of England was 'gay'
and by that logic I must also be 'gay'. I could imagine Fernando
secretly praying that Dudu was right.

I couldn't bask in the glory of my performance for too
long, as there was another training session starting at 4pm,
and I was expected to follow everybody else in enjoying a
siesta before then. The afternoon session was a training match.
Emerson joined in with the good-natured abuse I was receiving by
exploiting my ignorance of Portuguese.

Before the session, I had been encouraged by my team-
mates to call Emerson a *'viado'* – homosexual – and had to
pretend that I did not know what it meant. Not one to live and
let die, he stopped at the end of his pre-session pep talk:

Emerson: 'Sefi, *incomprehensible Portuguese suggesting 'are you
ready'.*

Seth: 'Yes' (thumb up to reinforce point).

Emerson: *Repeats in Portuguese* (pretending not to hear, hand
cupped to ear).

Seth: 'Yes!' (two thumbs up to doubly reinforce the point

- and I have heard it said that the thumbs-up in Brazil is an insulting gesture but everybody I met used it as the universal sign that everything was good).

Cue mass laughter amongst the Brazilians at my response. Yago, the sole fluent English speaker and one of the other few Sorriso residents, explained to me that Emerson had in fact asked if I was a homosexual, to which I had twice replied 'yes'. I joked to Emerson that we were no longer *amigos*.

The match itself was like all Brazilian matches I had experienced to date – baking hot and demanding with a constant feeling of impending death. On top of that my shins felt terribly exposed, after my normal shin pads were deemed to be too big ('Oh my God! What are these shields? I shall fight with these in the Coliseum, you understand, yes?' Yago had told me). I was given two pieces of plastic, about the size of my iPhone, which were meant to cover my whole legs.

The heat was the worst thing though. I would sweat when I ate in an air conditioned room it was that hot, so imagine the pain of being forced to sprint in the full glare of the sun. Even the boys from the more southerly areas of Brazil found the heat hard to handle. I was relieved when Emerson called for another left back, Charles, to replace me after 60 minutes, and subsequently appalled when the fitness coach Dauto called me over. I had to spend the rest of the session doing short, sharp sprints at the side of the pitch (stopping every time he looked away). Somehow I managed to escape the stadium without expiring, but I reckoned that it had been a close call.

A similar daily pattern followed throughout the week. Wake for breakfast and kit collection at 7.30am, train from 8.30-11, shower then eat lunch from 11.30-12.30. Then a siesta from 12.30-3.15pm before a final training session from 4-6.45. At the end of every session, we would have to do press-ups and sit-ups for a minimum of 10 minutes. Some would also stay and practice free kicks and ball work and no-one could leave until they were finished. Another shower would precede dinner at 7.30, and we would then be allowed free time, usually spent at an internet cafe, until bedtime, which was flexible. You just had to be back in the house by midnight.

Monitoring it all would be ever-present television cameras. They were fascinated by the pale English boy with the black boots. Such a plain colour was deemed unacceptable for Brazilians to wear – even white was pushing it.

Unfortunately for my health, harder sessions were to follow, though they must have believed I could take it as I passed my medical all the players were subjected to at the local hospital. They took basic data - weight, height, skin fold, lung capacity – as well as putting us through some basic movements and making us fill out paperwork. It took eight hours for us all to be tested.

The most punishing training was conducted in the sandbox in the city centre. Dauto took the session, which was focused on plyometrics – quick turns, explosive jumps and short sprints. Twelve stations were laid out, and we were expected to perform the tasks for two minutes each three times.

This torture was made worse by an ice cream seller cruelly deciding to set up next to our session. This resulted in around 30 locals attracted to watch us, all licking on deliciously cold ice creams whilst sat in the shade. Emerson had decided that he wasn't required for this session, but he still turned up halfway through, bag of shopping in hand accompanied by a bottle of refreshing water and Armani shades covering his eyes from the sun. The advertising board informed me that it was 48° Celsius – 118° Fahrenheit.

Oswaldo saved me that day. He would quickly respond to my desperate requests for water, and kept me just about hydrated enough to prevent me from collapsing. Oswaldo was full of

energy and laughter, not a bad bone in his body. He shared his
room in the house with Joaquim, who was significantly older
with his white hair. Indeed, all Joaquim needed was a beard to
complete the resemblance to a Brazilian Santa Claus, which was
topped off by his jolly laugh. Joaquim and Oswaldo had the
best deal in the house. Their room was about the same size as
mine but was only housing the two of them.

I had the second best deal, I had to admit, with just the five
others in my room – Pelezinho, Roger, a centre forward and
one of the older members of the squad, Chandler, Viniscius
and Michel. The room lodged between ours and the coaches
was slightly bigger than both but was home to eight Brazilians.
Even that wasn't the worst, however. A narrow bedroom that
ran the length of our rooms opposite the hallway had eight
bunk beds, though it was currently home to 'only' 15 people.

This meant that there were 31 living in Casa dos Filtros, 29
players and two staff. The other four players were locals and
lived at home. You could tell how overcrowded we were by the
state of the bathroom, though it was a relief at least that the
toilet brush had made its way back from the dining table to its
rightful place next to the toilet. The hygiene levels were truly
starting to affect me badly, and the cold trickle (when we were
lucky) that came out of the shower heads was barely enough to
wash my face.

I was spotty before I came to Brazil, but the pimples
that had previously occupied my face had now grown into
mountains of all shades and sizes. 'Monster, monster... Oh my
God, it is Shrek', greeted me every morning prior to my walk
to the bathroom to attempt to lessen them. No matter what I
did, however, they would just return with greater force the next
day.

Following a particularly sweaty morning session, Yago had
decided to shower at Casa dos Filtros with the rest of the team

instead of at his home. Usually I'd be too tired to move and would lie on my bed for a good 20 minutes after getting back from training. But I was feeling really hungry and decided to shower as soon as I got back. After a five-minute wait I was able to get under the freezing trickle and attempt to wash the sweat from my skin with the soap left at the shower.

'Oh man, what are you doing?' Yago asked.

'Washing.'

'Oh noo, no. This soap. The soap you use. How can I say? The guys, they use this to wash their ass holes with. It is like washing with this!' he said, pointing toward the sewage hole next to the back door.

I dropped the soap. All this time I had been washing my face with soap that the Brazilians used to wash their sweaty underwear with. No wonder I'd come up in spots, I'd be lucky if my face hadn't caught a sexually transmitted disease. The Brazilians were all laughing hysterically at me.

I was relieved that I had survived my first week of training. Now, after the horror of finding out about the soap, I was just glad that my face might start to get better.

5
WINDOW TO A NEW WORLD

Oswaldo was under strict orders from the coaches to bolt the front doors of Casa dos Filtros at midnight, though they remained unlocked during the day, almost inviting those from the favelas inside. Anyone caught breaking curfew was punished with having to clean the bathroom. But how could the Brazilians party if they had to be locked up in their rooms at midnight? Samba and partying was in their blood... The answer lay in my room.

The window, remember, was missing one of the bars designed to keep people out – or in. A slim body could just about fit through, and from there could jump up on to the wall and over the gate into the street. It meant that our window remained open all night to allow the more party-inclined (the majority) easy access and my room acted as the social hub of the house, with a steady stream of Brazilians coming and going. Usually there would be at least a couple going out, and more often than not the two were Chandler and Viniscius, who specialised in getting in at 5am. Sometimes they didn't even go to bed before morning training began.

Another of the Brazilians who enjoyed his excursions was Leo. Like much of the rest of the team, he was slightly built, particularly for a defender. He was edgy though, with a nose piercing and a scar on his face, and I soon came to see why he was known as the biggest character in the team. Part of that accolade came from his fondness for snorting cocaine and taking girls onto our team bus outside the house for sex.

On one occasion, early on in my stay and presumably after he'd taken something, I was loudly awoken at 4am, four and a half hours before morning training started. Leo had attempted to enter the window, but his current state meant that he ended up coming in head first which, if he was sober, would surely have been extremely painful. I only really got to see the full damage once he stood up. His white shirt was now red, stained by the blood gushing from several gashes on his body. He was missing a shoe, and a tooth as well, it seemed. He screamed a couple of words in Portuguese before running out of the room. Chandler, who had granted himself a rare night's sleep, let out an incredulous laugh before going back to sleep.

The true details of the Leo saga emerged only over the next couple of days, the first of them revealed on the team bus on the way to our morning session. 'Oh my God', came the cry from the first people to step on the bus as they held their noses in disgust. Despite his lack of sleep and the distinct probability that he was still drunk, Leo had made it to the bus for training. A big grin filled his face and he pushed those in front of him aside, racing to the back of the bus. He let out a volley of excitable words in Portuguese before frantically thrusting his pelvis on the backseat, simulating intercourse before pretending to ejaculate all over the seats. So that's why the bus smelt. Nobody sat on the back seats that morning though everyone congratulated Leo on his success.

Sex in Brazil is – how to describe it? – massive. The attitude to it is much more up-front and shameless than in England. It is everywhere. Nobody seemed to be bothered about what Leo had done but instead all were thrilled. So what if there was a bit of a spillage on the back seat? These things happened.

I had already witnessed this casual attitude in my first few days in Casa dos Filtros. We were given a rare afternoon off training, and I used it to visit the internet cafe, returning just before dinner. I walked into my room to find Michel sitting naked on the phone to his girlfriend. From what I could make out he was having quite passionate phone sex. Dudu was sitting on the bed opposite him reading a passage from his Bible as if nothing out of the ordinary was happening around him.

Heading into the bathroom did not mean escape from the scene either. There, Fernando stood naked in the shower masturbating. 'Sefi, today ten!' he shouted. He momentarily stopped playing with himself to hold up 10 fingers to illustrate his point. I tried not to look disgusted as I gave a thumbs up.

It was a daily ritual for Fernando to come and seek me out to tell me how many times he had pleasured himself that day. I wasn't sure why, but it didn't exactly make me feel comfortable. I liked him though. He was from the favelas in Rio de Janeiro and was desperately poor. He had already been at Casa dos Filtros for two months when I arrived, and had brought all of his belongings for the five months stay in a backpack: two vests, a pair of shorts, a toothbrush and a pair of football boots.

I had been surprised and delighted to find out that I would be paid 300 Reais a month – about £100 at that time – and when we received it at the end of the month (cash in hand, of course), Fernando would take out 50 Reais for himself and send the rest of the 300 back to his mother in Rio. His family had never seen such wealth, and Fernando took great pride in the fact that he was helping them to survive. I had never met anyone so happy before in my life. He was always smiling, laughing and joking, and became one of my good friends.

I had to wait a couple of days to discover the true extent of Leo's crazy night. My translator Yago had returned to training after heading to Cuiaba to sit some exams, and I sought him out in the warm-up jog round the pitch. 'Ohhh, Leo. That man is crazy!' said Yago, grinning. We both looked over at Leo, who still sported a large plaster on his face. I listened to Yago's story with incredulity.

Leo had gone to a party where he had taken drugs. At the party he had met several girls, and he especially liked the look of one. To his disgust, Leo couldn't find a spare room for himself and the girl, so in panic found a set of keys for one of the scooters that had been left outside. He rushed the girl onto the back of the scooter, instructing her to clutch onto him. He knew one place that was safe from prying eyes where he could get some privacy.

Breaking into the team bus located outside Casa dos Filtros was simple, mainly because the windows were always open. He crawled through the welcoming window to the back seat, lowering his hand to pull the girl up and into the bus. She successfully made it in, and she followed Leo to the back seat where they stripped off. After Leo had ejaculated all over the back seat the girl insisted that she had to go back to the party. Leo was disappointed as he wanted to go again, but he grudgingly agreed.

They got back onto the scooter and set off, the toxic mixture of alcohol and cocaine in Leo's body urging him to waste no time. Showing a complete disregard for red lights, he made it back quickly and dropped the girl off. There a big, surly man approached Leo, who had left the scooter at the side of the road. It was the girl's boyfriend, who immediately drew his fist back and landed an almighty punch into Leo's ribcage.

Leo was stunned but managed to hit back, and the pair were soon locked together, exchanging quick punches. The big, surly man floored Leo, and his friends began to join in. Leo, recognising that he was outnumbered, knew that he had to escape. The keys to the scooter were still in his pocket. He pushed the man, temporarily stunning him before making a run toward the scooter. He hopped on and rushed into the night air.

The man dived for Leo, but only succeeded in clutching thin

air. Leo was petrified. He couldn't think straight and he daren't look back or stop for a red light. A car came out of nowhere. It connected with the scooter, throwing Leo off in the process. The car hadn't been going fast but the scooter was still damaged beyond repair. The drink and the coke, in addition to the beating he had already received and the sheer fear and panic that the offended boyfriend would find him, nullified any of the pain that Leo was feeling. He knew he had to get back to safety, to Casa dos Filtros.

Before the driver could even get out of his car to check if he was OK, Leo was off, sprinting. Casa dos Filtros was not far away but surely his pursuer would not be far behind. Leo had a vague impression that he was missing a shoe, though he was not sure when he would have lost it. After 10 minutes of hard running, Leo made it to Casa dos Filtros. He scaled the wall with ease before diving head first into my room, concluding his night in the process.

I looked over at Leo, suitably impressed by his antics. What was more impressive was how Oswaldo and Joaquim seemed oblivious to the whole situation. He had got away with it! I guess if I had Leo on my team, I'd let him do what he wanted as long as it didn't affect him on the pitch. He was ridiculously talented. I was on Leo's team for the training session, him at right back, me at left back. Together we nullified the threat of Andrei and the also talented forward Roger, managing a clean sheet in the process.

* * *

I was beginning to find training more bearable but it was taking time. At Stamford we trained for three hours a week. Currently, I was training for 25. The Brazilian sessions were much more enjoyable, however. Training with Stamford would involve running around without a ball for the majority of the time before playing a short five-a-side game at the end. If we'd lost on the Saturday we might not even get to see a football. Here, everything was being done with the ball. Even when Emerson ordered us to do laps of the pitch we had to dribble a ball whilst running. Would a musician practise without his instrument? Would Van Gogh practise without his paint brush? That was Emerson's philosophy.

The one advantage of training with Stamford was the absence of a scorching sun, which remained an issue for me, but a few weeks in I could now just about manage to play a full match without feeling like keeling over. I no longer sweated when I ate, and generally felt more comfortable with the climate.

I was beginning to get used to the Brazilian style of play, and was becoming more comfortable making surging runs forward. I even managed to pull off a couple of nutmegs in the *Rondos* drill which began every single session. This drill saw the team form a circle with two people in the middle attempting to win the ball. The players on the outside of the circle were not permitted to take more than one touch at any time to keep the ball away. The player who lost the ball then had to go into the middle of the circle, replacing the man who had won the ball back.

I quickly learned that *Rondos* played a big part in creating the Brazilians' confidence and composure on the ball. The drill was hardly a foreign one; it is used regularly in England. The main difference is that in England the ball zips around the circle at 100 miles an hour. The players in the circle constantly look for that defence-splitting, million dollar pass. If you pass the ball to the player next to you then you are deemed a bad player who is shirking the responsibility of the next defence-splitting pass to a better, more technical player. Conversely, this means that the player rarely has to make a pass under pressure, and it promotes the idea that the ball is a hot potato which must be offloaded as quickly as possible.

In Brazil it is the other way round. The lesser players are the ones who offload the ball to the opposite side of the circle. The best players are the ones who draw in the pressure and play short passes to a man next to them, usually using the sole of the foot to do this. By drawing the defender in, the players not only learn to play under pressure, but also increase the chance of a nutmeg.

I lost count of the times I was in the middle of the circle. More often than not I'd get nutmegged – the ball being played between my legs. I couldn't help it, the technical superiority of the Brazilians was amazing. Nutmegs were celebrated more than goals – a ritual also evident in training games. Whenever a nutmeg occurred the whole practice stopped, allowing the man who performed the nutmeg to gloat, and the rest of the team to laugh at the poor victim. Even the centre backs would frequently pull off nutmegs.

I was beginning to see just how different football was in Brazil. It truly felt like a religion. It was in every area of life. Football is Brazil. Brazil is football. Brazilians talk of the game as an art, the nutmeg as a thing of beauty, and the coaches who teach the game are referred to as professors. Indeed, nobody called Emerson by his name in sessions, everyone called him 'Professor'.

Kids sacrifice all to become footballers. Daniel, for example, was a 13-year-old who had moved from his family in the Northern city of Belem to pursue his dream. He no longer went to school, he was too busy training. When we had finished the Copa São Paulo he would take some night classes, but for now football was the only thing on his mind.

Daniel was just as excited as the rest of us to learn that we would be playing our first friendly match in preparation for the Copa São Paulo in the next week, against the adult team that had won the Sorriso amateur league. Finally, a proper match instead of a training game.

I was excited; there had been a great deal of hype around me since my arrival, and I was well aware that there would be a lot of people eager to see my skills. The media had taken a great interest in me - I was interviewed almost daily, and there was always a radio station or television camera present at training – and this had inevitably rubbed off on the people of Sorriso.

Indeed, my teammates almost paraded me as a trophy whenever we walked around the city. 'Look, look, English!' they would inform, in excitable Portuguese, the gawping locals who would then come up to me and high five me or test out my ability to swear in the native tongue.

I just couldn't get over the attitude toward me, how foreigners were not only accepted but feted in Brazil. I suppose I should have known that Brazilians would be welcoming – their country does after all rely heavily on immigrants, was built on them indeed. In Sorriso alone there were thousands of Italian and German descendants, and Brazil as a whole has more black people than anywhere except Nigeria and more Japanese than anywhere outside of Japan.

Here I was, an Englishman from the nation who created football, coming to their small city to aid their quest for football dominance, and they were curious. Next week, they'd finally get to see to what extent I could help with that mission.

6
IT STARTED WITH A SAMBA

We were given the morning off from training ahead of our first match. None of the Brazilians had clambered through the hole in our window overnight, meaning that I was allowed a rare unpunctuated sleep. Despite this, Oswaldo sent me back to my bedroom after a breakfast of bread and chocolate Nesquik. We were all expected to spend the whole day resting, only emerging for mealtimes. The Brazilians took this command seriously – Dudu and Roger read their Bibles, Chandler and Michel slept, and Viniscius spent the time looking at photographs of himself (taken on my camera).

I decided to follow Dudu and Roger's lead and settled down with a book for the day. Alex Bellos's *Futebol*, an analysis of Brazilian football and culture, seemed like a good starting point and it gave me a lot of excellent background. I would also read *The Last King of Scotland* by Giles Foden, Khaled Hosseini's *The Kite Runner*, *Netherland* by Joseph O'Neill and Pele's autobiography while I was in Brazil.

Oswaldo came knocking on the doors at 3:30pm, telling us that it was time for a snack before leaving for the match. More than half of the Brazilians emerged from their rooms with a Bible in their hands. Some were reciting verses. This continued on the bus to the stadium, a bus which professed a religious message along its side – *'fica com Deus'*: stay with God - and which was also written in each room of Casa dos Filtros. The players were so immersed in the scriptures, indeed, that nobody shouted at the old unemployed men sat under their usual tree to *'vai trabalho'* (go to work) when we drove past, something that some of my team-mates usually did with great energy.

It was hot at the stadium, scorching in fact. We drove past a billboard that informed us it was 44 degrees. A small cluster of people was milling about in the stands, looking on interestedly as we wandered across the pitch towards the changing rooms. By the looks of it, we were the first people in the changing rooms for a while. The light did not work and there was broken glass everywhere. The small area of the room covered by natural light was soon filled by Brazilians eager not to sit on a rogue shard of glass. The rest of us had to jostle with the host of insects who were eagerly gorging on several chunks of watermelon. I didn't want to know how long the watermelon had been there.

Once we had managed to change we were told to gather in a circle. Dudu was wearing a T-shirt emblazoned with the message '100% Jesus'. About 10 of the players were either holding or wearing crosses. A Bible was placed in the middle of our circle. We stood, together with all of the coaches and technical staff, with our arms around each other and hands raised to the Heavens with our eyes closed whilst chanting the Lord's Prayer. Not wanting to upset the Brazilians, I joined in but in English.

After that came a communal prayer. They were not praying for victory – it would be pointless, as all Brazilian teams engage in this show of faith before games – but for God to watch over them and prevent them from getting injured. It prompted a strong surge of emotion throughout the team. After crossing themselves some looked up to the heavens, their arms still pointing upward, some hugged emphatically and a couple even kissed the Bible.

Religion is nearly as big as football in Brazil. Although the team were not all the same denomination of Christianity it was striking how seriously they all took their faith. Not one refused to profess their love of God. Indeed, almost 70% of the Brazilian population count themselves Roman Catholic, though Catholicism's grip over Brazil has been loosened by a surge of evangelical Protestantism. It is predicted that there are now more than 35 million Evangelicals in Brazil, out of a population of 200 million. Perhaps the most famous Brazilian Evangelical footballer was Kaka, who wore an 'I belong to Jesus' shirt under his match shirt when he played. I guessed that those who were most demonstrative in their expressions of faith – Dudu, Fernando and Roger – were definitely Evangelicals.

I had been named as a substitute and so retreated to the welcoming shade of the substitutes' bench as the starting 11 made their way on to the pitch. Most of the team crossed themselves and kissed the turf as they came out. The rest walked on with eyes closed and arms pointing to the skies. Michel kissed the penalty spot before taking his position in goal. The opposition – a local amateur team from Sorriso in a fluorescent lime green kit – were doing exactly the same.

About 500 people had gathered in the stand, along with the players who did not make the squad. They were joined by several TV cameras and a handful of reporters. There was a commentator positioned in the box, I presumed for Radio Sorriso. And they were treated to a fine performance from Emerson's team as we raced into a 3-0 lead.

I was thrilled to see my team-mates transfer the spontaneity they exhibited in training into a match. True, we were playing in a loose 3-5-2 formation, but it was so fluid, so unorganised. Gone was the rigid, disciplined system I had experienced in England (one former Stamford manager had screamed at me for crossing the halfway line in a game: 'What are you doing? Defenders defend. Now get the fuck back into your half!').

The players ghosted all over the pitch and appeared

comfortable anywhere. Vicente, a composed and intelligent holding midfield player from Cuiaba, was just as likely to be found at left back as playing up front, Chandler was regularly making lung-bursting runs forward from centre back. There didn't appear to be any clear instructions, just to get on the ball and create something and if that didn't work, try again. The game was slower than I was used to; more thoughtful, immeasurably more technical, more composed, yet just as aggressive.

The classic Brazilian ease with the ball was truly coming out, and it was quite obvious from the playful nature of our possessions that the team were enjoying themselves. Leo had certainly endeared himself to the crowd early on, turning round and using his buttocks to lob cheekily a pass over his marker's head to Roger.

I, on the other hand, was feeling overcome by nerves. My team was good. A bit too good for my liking. I was going to stick out terribly. All of the media hype surrounding me would turn out to be false. I would be found out by the watching locals, my shortcomings immortalised by the video recordings of the game. I was sweating heavily.

As the second half began, Dauto led us all over to an area behind our goal. It is common practice in Brazil for substitutes to spend the whole of the second half warming-up. When I was a substitute in England, the subs' warm-up would consist of a couple of strolls up and down the touchline at around 60 minutes before standing and talking to supporters, making sure I was stretching every time the manager looked over. The Brazilian method could not have been further from what I was comfortable with. Dauto had us training to run the marathon and there was no letting up. If any of us walked or attempted to watch the game, we would get shouted at and ordered to continue.

I was so happy when Emerson called my name to tell me

that I was about to be substituted on to the pitch that I forgot
all of my nerves. The roar from the crowd as they saw me putting on my match shirt was thrilling. The game stopped and I
replaced Furlan, a local boy who felt great pride in, and commitment to, the club, running over to take my position on the
left flank, on the stand side right next to the fans.

A chant of *'Inglese! Inglese!'* greeted me. A cheer greeted my
first touch, a simple pass back to Chandler at centre half. The
cheers soon turned into comments, notably led by my team-
mates in the stands. 'Your sister, she is beautiful', 'Hey *Inglese*, I
marry your sister', 'Sefi gay!'

I didn't care. I had never received such attention. My final
game in England before coming to Brazil was played in front of
62 rather bored spectators, including the stereotypical man and
his dog, at Market Drayton Town. Compared to that this was
incredible – there were loud chants, dancing in the stands and
even a couple of flares. (Mind you, against Market Drayton, I
did at least have the pleasure of playing down the left-hand side
with one of my childhood heroes, the former Peterborough
United player David Farrell).

About 10 minutes into my debut, just as I thought I was
getting the hang of the game, the inevitable happened. I was
nutmegged, much to the delight of the crowd who were loud
in their mocking. Another loud person was our central midfielder Charles, just 15 but physically mature and not lacking in
confidence, who managed to pick up two yellow cards within
10 seconds, both for dissent. The whole nature of the game
changed after this, and our goal was bombarded for the final
10 minutes of the game. Our 10 men stood firm, however, and
we rode out 3-0 winners. I was given a standing ovation by the
crowd as I went over to clap them, and I even made out an 'I
love you Sefi' in between the relentless shouts of affection for
my sister.

Back in the changing rooms we gathered for a final prayer to thank God for watching over us and keeping us safe before heading back across the pitch to the team bus.

'Oh man, all the guys, they say you run very much', Yago told me. I thought that this was a compliment. I was greeted with several more compliments on my way to the bus. A few of the spectators had stayed behind to wait for us, and several of these were friends of Andrei. One was very keen to seek me out to speak to me. Cassius had spent a couple of unhappy years living in London.

'I hate London, it is all work, work, work, no play,' he said. 'The weather, it is cold, the people, they are cold. It is a cold place. It is much more friendly in Brazil'. I couldn't help but agree with him.

I had obviously endeared myself to Andrei's friends, and they invited me to a big party that they were throwing that weekend. I was only allowed to get on the bus once I had promised them I would attend. And on the bus, the Bibles were out again, along with the instruments that always accompanied the shouting at the unemployed men under the tree on our journeys through town. There were always two sets of hand drums, and a couple of players would use the empty water drums to add to the music. Everybody sang. I sat back and considered what Cassius had said. He was right: I could not have come to a friendlier, happier place. England was cold, Brazil warm. Oswaldo handed me a drum.

The Chairman welcomed us back at Casa dos Filtros with a table full of pizza. It was possibly the best thing I had seen since being in Brazil. Until then, the food had been exactly the same in the house every day: rice and flavourless beans for both lunch and dinner, accompanied by the saltiest, toughest beef requiring a strong jaw to work it into digestible chunks. Sometimes, if we were lucky, we would be given beetroot. The food was so bland that I even began to join the Brazilians in drinking an espresso after a meal. I hated coffee, but it least it had flavour.

After a couple of slices of the wondrous pizza the Chairman took me to one side. First of all he congratulated me on my performance, then he told me of a 'problem', saying that my team-mates had been eyeing up my belongings for themselves. 'They want it for gift, be careful,' he warned me. After this temporary downer he followed with much more positive news, promising me that he would sign me as a professional player following the Copa São Paulo. I returned to my colleagues, who were watching the highlights of our match on the local news channel, with a beam that remained on my face all night.

We were given another morning off training, and I got up late following our celebrations the previous night. I wandered in to the kitchen to find my team-mates gathered around the small television in the kitchen. It was December and the draw for the following summer's World Cup finals in South Africa was taking place. A huge boo greeted the announcement of England's name, with a torrent of abuse aimed at me, my personal favourite being 'David Beckham sucks the dick of Brazil!' The cameras flashed to an image of Beckham, who was sporting a new Mohican haircut. Chandler, Roger and Fernandao, an 18-year-old with the maturity of a 30-year-old, all arrived at afternoon training with the same Mohican hairstyle. The worldwide influence of Beckham was just as evident in Brazil as anywhere else.

The Brazilians naturally insisted that their own World Cup in four years time would be the tournament of all tournaments and we would finally see true football. Of course Brazil would win it, they insisted and the whole world would see what a wonderful country they lived in. It was before they and many others in Brazil came to see the lavishness of it all and costs rising as

standards of living fell, resentment growing among the population towards the government.

We left Casa dos Filtros to get the bus for afternoon training
to find the Chairman in an animated row with the bus driver.
The subject of unpaid wages seemed to crop up. After a couple of minutes the Chairman pointed down the street and the
driver stormed off. This was the third driver that the Chairman,
clearly not a man to be crossed, had sacked in the month I had
been here. There was a delay of 20 minutes as the Chairman
went through his phone book to choose the next lucky candi-
date to take the poisoned chalice of SEC bus driver.

It had been raining heavily throughout the day, which made
the trip to training quite tricky for the new driver, especially
as some roads were heavily flooded. '*Vamos motorista*' went the
cries from the back seat of the bus, with Chandler playing
a suitably rapid tune on the water drums to emphasise their
desire for him to speed up. The new driver resisted, and the
boys soon lost interest, instead turning their attention to the
unemployed men sheltering from the rain under their trees.

The rain stopped just before the bus arrived at the stadium
but looking at the pitch, I wasn't sure how we could train. Both
goalmouths were covered with standing water and there were
small ponds all over the pitch. In England there was no chance
that it would have been played on. I was in Brazil, however, and
Yago informed me that 'man, this pitch is no problem. In Brazil
we play on much worse'.

The session had been scheduled as a training match. It wasn't
very competitive as both goalkeepers were forced to stand on
the edge of their 18-yard box, making the lob shot a great goal-
scoring method. After four lobbed goals in 15 minutes, making
the score 2-2, the inevitable happened and the heavens opened
once again. We spent five minutes trying to play on but it was
hopeless. We could hardly see across the pitch and Emerson

eventually whistled and we frantically ran for cover, straight onto the bus.

I went to Yago's house that evening. Originally of Italian extraction, he was from Florianopolis in the South of Brazil, but his extended family all lived in Sorriso. He was staying with his grandparents, who had a large gated house. Yago's aunt lived in one of the houses next to this, and his uncle ('He's in the Government. Man, they are all crooked') lived on the other side. On the other side of that was one of Yago's cousins and another one lived next door to that.

What was remarkable to me about the houses – though it was not unusual in Brazil – was their proximity to the despairing poverty of favelas. All of the houses were spacious, all were gated, and most had swimming pools. Yet not even 50 yards from Yago's cousins' house was a decrepit shanty town, with small huts built from any materials that the owner could find. Most had corrugated iron roofs. Few were bigger than my room in Casa dos Filtros. The street summed up Brazil with its sheer extremes of wealth and poverty.

I had been spending quite a lot of time at Yago's. He would pick me up from Casa dos Filtros in a large 4x4 before transporting me across town. 'If there is accident not my fault', he had told me the first time he picked me up. I asked him what age you needed to be to drive in Brazil. '18' came the proud response. Yago was 16.

Going to Yago's house was a welcome break from Casa dos Filtros – I was able to have a warm shower ('Look, warm water!' Yago had excitedly exclaimed when he first showed me), speak in my native language and eat something other than rice and beans, food that actually tasted of something. He proudly referred to himself as my 'Google translate', with his fluency in both English and Brazilian Portuguese being highly useful.

As a player, he was not typically Brazilian, either on or off the pitch. He was quite pale and lanky, not particularly athletic looking and was not the most co-ordinated on the pitch. A roaming striker, ball control and dribbling were not his strongest points. Later he would become a centre back and would thrive. He had become my best friend. Always fond of a laugh and a joke, he was a positive character. We had a similar sense of humour, and spent many hours bonding over our love of American comedies.

He had recently introduced me to his female cousin, Tangrianne, who lived two doors away. On our first meeting we had gone off driving two buggies around Sorriso. Yago insisted that Tangrianne and I share a buggy. She was 19, a year older than me, and had recently spent time in England at a Cambridge University summer school where she had acquired an ability to speak a broken, disjointed form of English. I had had an unsuccessful interview at the university the previous year, which gave us both enough to talk about to break the ice.

We were laughing for the majority of the journey, and Yago was beaming when we got back to his house. 'Ahh, you like her, man? She is a beautiful girl, no?' he asked me.

Since then Yago had ensured that Tangrianne was always at his house when I was around. She looked archetypically Brazilian. Whereas the majority of Yago's family were rather pale, probably due to their Italian roots, Tangrianne's skin was olive, her hair long, black and flowing. Her dark eyes were prominent, their long eyelashes inviting you to gaze deep into her beauty. She had a gentle tone of voice which was both endearing and warm. She welcomed me with her usual warm hug, before quickly directing me toward some chocolate and pizza. I was pleased that she understood what I wanted. I had recently seen her in a bikini. We swam for hours.

Yago turned the television on and loaded an Ali G episode that we had not yet watched. Ali G was Yago's favourite

programme. He had watched it continuously during his adoles-
cence, and the 'Jafaican' accent that Ali G used had combined
with the American English Yago had been taught at his private
school to give him a quite unique accent. Tangrianne sounded
more Eastern European.

Talk soon got on to the big party that Andrei's friends were
throwing, which, for some reason, had been named *Feijoada*
after the rice and bean dish which had so tormented my stay
in Brazil. It seemed that the party was a big event in Sorriso.
Tangrianne was eager to know that I would be there. I
promised her I would. I wasn't sure if Yago or Tangrianne was
more delighted with the news. '*Eyyyyy, festa! Festa! Festa!*' Yago
hollered, dancing up and down. Tangrianne smiled. Yago had
run to the laptop to load up YouTube. He quickly clicked on to
a 'rebelation' video – a new Brazilian dance craze.

'Hey man, if you come to a party, you need to learn to
samba, OK? Tangrianne will show you how', said Yago.
Tangrianne smiled as she led me through the dance. Samba is
almost as important as football in Brazil. In fact, there seems
to be an unwritten law that all Brazilian natives must be able to
samba, and it is thought that the lively, rhythmic dance, with its
emphasis on the movement of the hips, is pivotal, along with
feijoada, to the reasons why Brazilians play football with such
flair, passion and creativity. Tangrianne had her gentle hands on
my awkward hips. We were close and I could smell her perfume
as I stared into those deep, dark eyes. Yago was beaming with
pride.

7
PARTIES AND PUNCH-UPS

This afternoon, for a change, the team bus was not heading to training. Andrei's friends had commandeered it and hired a driver to take the team to their party. We had had a hard morning session – a *físico*, which included long-distance runs and numerous sprints before we were transferred to the dreaded sandbox to complete a few circuits. The sand was so hot even at that time of the day that Oswaldo had to hose it down with water before anybody was able to bear walking on it. The session was so hard that Emerson gave us the rest of the day off, quite handy given that the party began in the early afternoon.

The driver dropped us off at a house near the sandbox in the city centre. It was a tall, white complex that looked like something you'd find in California rather than South America. This was Cassius's house, and he energetically greeted us, ushering us past the four bouncers hired to guard the doors. We walked in to a large courtyard packed with people, most of whom were wearing 'official' white *Feijoada* T-shirts. The walls were all white, the chairs too. There was a swimming pool in one corner of the complex, a 4x4 in the other. The three portaloos in the far corner seemed out of place in comparison to these riches. The well-stocked bar was located against the back wall and was side-by-side with a barbecue. Andrei had brought two of his father's finest pigs, both of which were being spit-roasted, to the delight of the watching Brazilians.

Andrei lived with his parents on a farm on the outskirts of Sorriso, amid a part of rainforest which the workers must have forgotten to clear when they built Sorriso. It was tradition to spend Sunday afternoons on Andrei's farm. We had been there every Sunday since I had arrived in Brazil, and it was what I most looked forward to each week. A forest of mango trees stood to attention to greet the team bus as it made its way down the long driveway. From the bus, we all went in different directions, some to select which pig we would like to eat, some to pick the fresh mangos from the trees, the rest to swim in the river.

I usually opted for the river. It was the most calming sensation I had ever experienced. The air was so fresh. It tasted of fruit and told of health. And it was so quiet, save for the distant chirp of insects. We would dive in and let the current take us away, floating on our backs and observing the beautiful scenery that surrounded us. I once saw a spider's web which must have been the size of a small bungalow. It was fascinating.

Occasionally we would float to an island on the far bank from the wooden diving board that Andrei's father had built. Once we had clambered onto the island, we would explore, spotting tropical wildlife and foraging for fruit. It was even more peaceful in this small patch of rainforest. Civilisation seemed so far away, a world away from the 'cold' hustle and bustle of England with its 'work, work, work and no play' culture. The only interruptions would be the distant squeal of the pigs as Andrei's father slaughtered them.

I was glad that the pigs had already been killed before I arrived at *Feijoada*. I always felt so guilty when hearing their desperate squeals pierce the calm air. Their delicious taste always alleviated the guilt. I headed straight for the food, eager to be rid of the bland taste of rice and beans we had lunched on. Andrei was there with Furlan and Luis, both of whom were also Sorriso residents in our team. They were all wearing official *Feijoada* T-shirts, which appeared to be helping them to attract plenty of female attention.

They soon deflected the female attention towards me, by pointing out that I was English. The girls were suddenly transfixed, holding on to my every word. I wished I could be like this in England. These girls didn't even notice my big nose, and seemed oblivious to the fact that there were still white spots dotted around my face following my major soap error. After my timid 'hello' I realised that I had no idea how to keep the girls entertained. Leo leant over to me, and whispered something in my ear. I repeated what he had said to the girls. They giggled, looked at me and turned away. Everyone else was crying with laughter. Yago had heard and came over, tears streaming down his face too but for another reason.

'Hey man, why you ask those girls to make a baby with you? My cousin not good enough for you?' he asked, hurt. Leo assured him that I was in need of his help and he was only trying to do what was best. He looked at me with disdain, '*Inglese* is much bad with the girls'.

Leo wasn't bad with the girls. Nor was Michel, who had made an extra special effort to attract female attention. He had done something in his eyes, and the pupils were both now a brilliant shade of blue in addition to being twice the usual size. The Brazilians had been unforgiving with their abuse, and they made me refer to him as '*olho bonita*' – beautiful eyes – at every opportunity. Michel didn't care, and he had been fluttering his eyelashes at anything and everything with a pulse. Eventually a girl had taken an interest and they had gone off together. 'Ugliest girl here,' Leo had muttered with a slight hint of jealousy. I wondered if Michel still had his girlfriend back home.

Leo wasted no time in attempting to match Michel. Like Michel he had been trying to seduce every single female within the vicinity, but he now made an extra special effort. Leo was very drunk by this stage and was slurring his words. We had only been here an hour.

He seemed to take offence when he was rejected by yet another girl, and he refused to take no for an answer. A man stepped in to try and move Leo, but still he persisted. The man swung a punch at Leo, who was too inebriated to react quickly enough to get out of the way, and hardly had much ability to balance left. He fell and suddenly there were punches being thrown everywhere. The whole area around the house had descended into a punch-up, with the security guards employed hopelessly understaffed and unable to prevent it.

After about five minutes the fight subsided, and security ejected several people. Leo was somehow spared. Unperturbed, he bounced up to his feet and looked to seek out his next target, an overweight woman who must have been at least 10 years his senior. I knew that these were his speciality. We had argued over it when we first entered the party.

'Look at her,' he had said to me, pointing to a portly figure with long hair, 'She is beautiful. Why don't you make sex with her?' Leo, like most of the Brazilians, was very blunt and straight to the point. I had taken one look at her and had not particularly liked what I saw.

'No, no, she is too fat,' I replied. 'Too fat!' Leo had an incredulous look on his face. 'Man, you must be gay. You should go make sex with Elias.' I looked over at Elias, a local governor of Sorriso who doubled up as a director at SEC. He was dancing a quick samba in a big crowd of females, a look of sheer delight on his face. You could quite easily tell his sexual orientation. He didn't hide it. He was openly gay.

Many of the Brazilians shared Leo's views. Whereas slimness is seen as the desirable female trait in England, Brazilian men like their women to be curvaceous. From what I could make out, the especially curvy parts that they deemed desirable were the breasts, hips and bottom, and when a female began to samba, these would all playfully jiggle about. Leo seemed to value a curvaceous belly more than anything.

My team-mates had spent most of the party attempting to get me to 'make sex' with the girls. I had spoken with many of them (all were keen to speak to someone with an English accent; it seemed that it was more desirable to be English than to be a footballer), but had quickly realised that after greeting them with a 'hello' and asking them how they were, I did not have much of an ability to sustain a conversation. The only Portuguese I knew was swear words, football terminology and a sex song that Leo had taught me.

And so it was that I asked endless females how they were before looking a bit nonplussed about what to say next. They must have looked at this poor, timid 18-year-old foreigner with a bit of despair, and after politely waiting for me to stumble over my poorly pronounced words, moved on. All the while my team-mates became more and more fraught.

I was glad when Tangrianne arrived. There had been another fight just before her arrival, but it involved fewer people and the security guards were able to throw out the culprits quickly and efficiently. The complex was by now a bit untidy and I had lost quite a few of my team-mates. Finally I'd be able to speak to a girl in peace, to ask her more than how she was feeling without being surrounded by Brazilians ordering me to make sex with her.

Many of them had lost interest by now, and Chandler, Michel, Roger (obviously forgetting the photographs of his girlfriend he had stuck all around our room), Fernandao and Furlan had all found female partners and disappeared. Not wanting to be outdone by anyone, Viniscius was desperately searching around the complex. Leo was doing exactly the same, but his movement had slowed down as the alcohol affected him more and more.

There weren't many of my team-mates around now and I felt isolated without my Google translate, Yago. I wasn't sure where he had gone. Tangrianne greeted me, and engaged me in conversation briefly before excusing herself to say hello to some old friends. She looked beautiful. Her scent was still in the air as Elias pounced on me.

'Sefi!' he said, embracing me as if we were the best of friends. 'Why aren't you dancing, beautiful?' Oh, no. He's called me beautiful. What do I do? I was panicking. The boys had all joked about me being gay because I didn't like large girls. I hoped that they hadn't said anything to him. I needed a distraction, to think of something quickly.

'I don't know how to samba', I mumbled. At least, I think that's what I said. 'I don't know' was one of the few phrases that I knew how to say. Elias beamed: 'It's easy', he said, positioning himself behind me and placing his hands on my hips, 'follow me'. I'd dug the hole deeper. A couple of my team-mates had clocked what was going on. They weren't coming to help. They were too busy pointing and laughing.

THWACK. The sound of a punch was followed by a piercing shriek. Suddenly everyone was fighting. Thankfully, my distraction had arrived. I rushed to the corner of the complex, one of the only areas that the fight had not yet reached. The security guards now had batons, but there were just too many people to stop.

I spotted Leo in the middle of the scene. He had punched someone before diving into the swimming pool. The victim was prowling round the edge, waiting for him to climb out of the pool. Leo was sticking his finger up at him. Fernando and Leandro were near me, and I managed to reach them without having to engage in a fight. The three of us watched on with incredulity for a good 10 minutes. Then the police arrived. They made short work of the fight, aggressively clearing the scene in minutes. Cassius stood on a table and announced that the party was over. It wasn't even 5pm, we had barely been at the party for three hours. It was supposed to go on until 5am.

'Oh, man, what a party!' said Yago, returning from wherever he had been hiding himself. He had seen the whole altercation that sparked the final fight. One of his cousins had not liked the way a man was looking at Tangrianne, and had let him know his feelings with a strong punch to the stomach. Unfortunately the man on the end of the punch had a whole group of friends with him and they reacted badly to this protective act by Yago's cousin, sparking the mass brawl. I was told they were fairly standard at Brazilian parties.

I couldn't see Tangrianne anywhere and was disappointed that I had got to spend so little time with her. Yago had to pack to go back home to Florianopolis the next day, which meant that I had to return to Casa dos Filtros with the rest of the team. I would have to wait to see Tangrianne.

From *Feijoada* the party, it was back to earth with *feijoada* the meal and more rice and beans at Casa dos Filtros. After that, those of us who were still sober enough decided to head to a local bar to play snooker. The bar of choice was a brisk 10-minute walk away, at the edge of the local favela. It was doing a roaring trade and the street was packed with Brazilians dancing and drinking. I was glad that I had not brought my phone out with me.

It felt like everybody was staring at me; the foreigner, the sole white face. 'He must be rich,' they seemed to be thinking. I let Luciano get me a drink. He was a tall and physically impos-ing centre half from Cuiaba with bloodshot eyes that gave him an intimidating look until you got to know him. I felt safest at the snooker table and my nerves soon subsided as I began to play. Luciano partnered me and his hit-and-hope tactics propelled us to victory after victory. Tangrianne was no longer in my mind. Fewer people were staring at the foreign white kid. Nobody had killed me. I was safe.

I returned to Casa dos Filtros a happy man, unlike the Chairman who was on the premises and on the prowl. His face contorted in to a rage that he subsequently unleashed on me as soon as I stepped through the front door.

'SEFI! WHAT YOU DOING! WHAT! WHY? NO! NO! NO!' he screamed at me as I stood rooted to the spot, trapped. Everybody else had scarpered in to their rooms. 'SEFI, NO! You no go Three Street. Bad people. City – fine. No problem. Casa dos Filtros – OK. Three Street – bang bang, confusion, murder. Soccer player – big problem. Bang bang. Understand?!'

I must have looked scared because the Chairman had lowered his voice. He no longer seemed as angry. I felt empathy for those poor bus drivers who had gotten on the wrong side of him. I gave him a timid nod. It seemed that I had been lucky to escape with my life. He smiled and beckoned for me to return to my room. I was only too happy to accept his invitation.

Chandler was the only person in my room. Michel and Roger were still with the girls they had met. Dudu and Viniscius were playing cards in the next room. Nobody had seen Leo. Chandler put his arm round me.

'OK?' he said with a smile. 'Ah', he got his laptop and loaded up the internet. He clicked on to Google translate and began to write. It came out in translation as: 'If you ever need help ask me anything. Protect your stuff. I look out for anything. The others are scared of me'. Yago had repeated Viniscius's rumour that Chandler had spent time in prison. I wasn't sure how he had such a reputation. He was one of the most welcoming people in Casa dos Filtros.

Chandler continued to type. He told me of his home in the South, of how he played for Internacional of Porto Alegre, a Serie A club, before signing for Sorriso, and how it was his dream to play football in Europe, a dream that had intensified after seeing me come to Brazil to play. I promised him I would do my best to help. We embraced, and spent the rest of the evening football freestyling in the tiny space in our room. Before we went to sleep he told me that he loved me.

8
MIND GAMES

Waking up was still horrible. The ridiculous amount of training that my body was being put through ensured that I awoke each morning in a state of near rigor mortis. It took at least five minutes to get out of bed, my body always begging me not to rise, my brain (and Oswaldo) always insisting that I must. I'd sigh to myself, realising that not even professional footballers could have it all.

Emerson worked us hard – the Copa São Paulo was of overwhelming importance, not only to the football club, but to the whole city who had shown us such support. The youth team was entered every year in the state championship, which ran from January until April, and had done well to win the title but only when resources allowed them to recruit better players did they enter the Copa. I would later discover that more than 300,000 Reais – £100,000 – had been invested in us. We owed them.

Given this, it was not out of the ordinary for Emerson to put us through sprint training, a 60-minute match, position-specific training and keep-ball drills in a single session, often lasting more than two-and-a-half hours. This alone would be far more than my body could manage, but most days it would be subjected to two of these sessions.

As a full back my schedule was particularly heavy. The Brazilian philosophy could not have been more different from the English 'defenders should defend and that's that'. Here, the full back was expected to be up and down the pitch the whole game. In Emerson's formation the full backs were the only players who occupied the flanks of the pitch, placing huge importance on them. None of the training drills I performed was defensive. I was encouraged to spend as much time in the attacking half as possible. My training drills consisted solely of crossing the ball or shooting from range.

Inevitably the vest that Oswaldo gave me to wear would end up soaked in sweat. Even the other Brazilians complained of the heat, many of them from the South, where the temperature is more European, and those from from São Paulo found it almost unbearable. It was not uncommon for us to have to train in humid conditions with temperatures touching 50° Celsius. I guess this is why we were given such salty beef. Oswaldo also distributed a variety of tablets after each session, each designed to replace the minerals that we had lost by the bucket load in our sweat.

The Copa São Paulo was slowly sneaking up on us. We played another three friendly games against adult teams from the area, including one from Sinop and one from Lucas do Rio Verde, adding a 2-2 draw and 3-1 and 7-0 wins to our inaugural 3-0 victory.

I still managed to get nutmegged in the 7-0. Despite this I was getting used to playing on pitches that either had no grass or far too much grass. I got my first assist in the 3-1 victory, and it seemed like everyone congratulated me for it. The media rushed to speak with me afterwards, despite the fact that Roger, a muscular physical presence and a good finisher, had scored a hat-trick.

'Much happy,' I told them, thumbs up to illustrate my point. This was a slight lie; I could have had my first goal in the same game, but Rian had shot from a tight angle instead of squaring the ball to me when I had an open goal at my mercy. I shouldn't have been surprised, though. You could tell from his 14 stone frame that he was pretty greedy.

Rian emerged from the games as one of our best players. He was only 15, but his weight gave him great strength and he had a wicked turn of pace. Rian had probably given up more than anybody else to be here. Despite his youth, he had a child back in Rio who had just reached his first birthday. He no longer attended school. He was not academic and football was his only chance of providing for his child. He was hungry and it showed, on and off the pitch. I always made sure I stocked up on my salty beef and, on rare occasions, spaghetti before Rian served himself.

Chandler was also a favourite of Emerson. He was assured at centre half and very composed on the ball. Luis, meanwhile, had been given the captaincy. He was a combative central midfielder and also the Club President's son but he deserved to be the leader of the team. Stocky and imposing on the pitch but also highly approachable off it, he also exhibited the pride and commitment of a local boy playing for his club.

Luis's 13-year-old brother Leozinho also played in the team, though he still attended school in Sorriso and did not make every session. I was pleased for Luis, who had invited me to his home several times. He always made sure that his mother cooked me spaghetti when I visited.

Unlike Yago, Luis had satellite television which showed English football matches. I was amused to hear Brazilian commentators referring to Rooney as 'Shrek', rather than by his surname. There was something poetic about the commentator excitedly yelling 'GOOOOOOOOL, GOL DO SHREK, ROONEY!'

Not everyone was happy about Luis being captain, notably Viniscius. But then, Viniscius thought that he should not only be captain of Sorriso, but captain of Brazil. Granted, he was good, but he was the most egotistical person in the team by a long way. Staying in the same room as him was beginning to test my patience. When he wasn't on his nightly forages through the window, he was staying up till the early hours of the morning, playing his music – and he always got to choose it – loudly. It was the culture to play samba music non-stop when we weren't training, but Viniscius didn't seem to understand the need to turn it down when people wanted to sleep.

Lately he had developed an obsession with me. If I had been out I would usually return to find him either sleeping in my bed, wearing my clothes, using my iPhone, taking pictures with my camera or just plainly searching through my belongings. When he came back drunk from his forages he would usually try and wake me by tickling my feet or trying to steal my boxers. Once I took a swing at him. I was glad that I missed. Viniscius was much bigger than me, and in retrospect it seemed wise not to have him feeling like he owed me a punch. Thankfully he was too drunk to remember.

In the days leading up to Christmas, training became more informal. Luis's 24-year-old brother Fabrice turned up to train with the team. The new bus driver had a huge row with the Chairman prior to Fabrice's session and, like his predecessor, stormed off. Not to worry, Fabrice said, he had driven a car before and how much harder could it really be to drive a bus?

It took him several minutes to work out how to turn on the engine and even longer to work out how to make the bus go. '*Vamos motorista*' came the gleeful cry from the back seat. I prayed that he would ignore them. He didn't. We were going faster and faster, and all the while the Brazilians were demanding that Fabrice put his foot down further. Red lights would not even slow him down; indeed, it seemed that they made him go faster. Cars beeped their horns. 'Wahey' came the cry from the back seat as Roger blew kisses at the angry drivers.

Momentarily the Brazilians were distracted from roaring on Fabrice. There was an attractive girl walking along and Fabrice slammed on the brakes. A good 10 players leaned out of the windows, hollering at the *gostosa bonita* as the bus trundled past. 'We make sex, no?' Dudu shouted. 'Your breasts are beautiful, *caramba*!' Leo was full of compliments. This was nothing out of the ordinary. It happened every time we drove past a female of any description. It was almost as regular as shouting at the unemployed men under their tree, as playing the drums and empty water holders, as samba-ing down the aisle.

As soon as the girl was out of sight, Fabrice put his foot down once more. Although not particularly religious, I said a little prayer and crossed myself once we pulled up at the training pitch. Fabrice turned round to me, his face a picture of pure delight. 'I farted,' he informed me, the only English that he knew, before picking up his football boots and exiting the bus. He forgot to turn the engine off.

The session started with a game of chain tag – one chasing the group and everyone linking up until the last one is caught – as a warm-up before a multi-sided match, the coaches joining in. Rules were, of course, imposed. We were only able to use our left foot in the first half, and our right foot in the second half. Use of the wrong foot resulted in a free kick for the other team. Viniscius and Dudu went in goal for either team and were both awful, even worse than Oswaldo was on the pitch. They were so bad that even I managed to score a goal (diving header, bullet).

Most of the game was spent attempting to stay on the opposite side of the pitch to Emerson, who was especially fond of producing dangerously high and badly-timed slide tackles. Fabrice, unlike Oswaldo, was surprisingly good considering his resemblance to a hairy round ball and his chain-smoking regimen. It was a shame that he could only play for 10-minute bursts. He still managed to nutmeg me. 'I farted! I farted!' he roared in celebration.

The drive back from training was just as life-threatening as the drive to, the Brazilians daring Fabrice just as much and the red lights deemed just as pointless. Once again I crossed myself when we arrived safely at Casa dos Filtros. This time Fabrice managed to turn the engine off before leaving the mobile death trap.

We were greeted in the dining area by the rare sight of the main coaching staff, who were accompanied by the Chairman and a man I had never seen before. He must have been in his 30s, and was perhaps even paler than me. He was evidently a good friend of the Chairman, who spent at least 10 minutes introducing him.

I soon discovered that the Chairman's friend was a nutter. I think his official title was 'Team Psychologist', but his methods were definitely questionable. Within two minutes he was ordering us to jump around celebrating as if we had just won the World Cup. He then made us repeat this whilst chanting 'SEC! SEC! SEC!'

After all of this exercise we were told to sit down in a circle and hold hands. With eyes closed we had to chant repeatedly – with the nutter's encouragement – '*SEC melhor time do mundo*' (SEC are the best team in the World), with each repetition ordered to be louder. This lasted 10 minutes before the nutter decided to slow things down. We were still in our circle, and we now had to follow him in clicking our fingers repeatedly. We then had to shout '*buhu*' (stupid) at our leisure. I didn't understand why.

Following this, he began a lengthy speech, the gist of which seemed to be that we were very good players and could match anybody on our day. Maybe everyone who didn't play for SEC was *buhu*. He finished his session by making us hug every one

of our team-mates to ask for forgiveness. I wasn't quite sure
for what. 'Oh man, this guy, he crazy!' an excitable Andrei
remarked before our hug. I could only agree.

After an hour, the nutter was finally moved on. The
Chairman once again took the spotlight, thanking his friend for
a quite inspirational session. He called Emerson, who had given
out particularly forceful hugs, to join him to perform the SEC
Christmas bonanza. All of our names were placed into Emerson's England cap. The first name to be pulled out was to be
rewarded with 200 Reais – nearly a month's wages. The second
would get 100 Reais and the third and final name 50.

It seemed that the near unbearable temperature outside was
unable to melt any Christmas spirit, as Emerson's fingers were
drawn to the slip with Fernando's name on. Fernando bounded
up to collect his prize, all of which I later learned he sent the
next day to his family. Well, nearly all. First he treated himself
to an ice cream. In contrast to Fernando's generosity, Viniscius
refused to pay me the 10 Reais he owed me despite being the
second name that Emerson called. Apparently he needed it to
buy even more clothes.

Everyone was in the Christmas mood after the bonus
bonanza, particularly after the Chairman presented each player
with a box of chocolates, as well as 50 Reais as a seasonal gift.
In celebration, the window not fully barred was in high demand
that evening, and I would make my first use of it. A few of the
younger members of the team decided to head to an ice cream
parlour, and Fernando and I joined them. Fernando only had a
single scoop before heading off to a church in the nearby area
to say his thanks for receiving such a gift.

The rest of us went to the ten pin bowling alley where we
were greeted by a group of girls that Daniel had befriended.
Guessing that they were likely to be a similar age to Daniel, I
knew that I had to be very careful. I had been taught a lot of

incriminating phrases, and I would have to avoid using them. Bruno, one of the four goalkeepers in the squad, did not share my caution, and he was only halfway through the first game before he was kissing a girl with braces on her teeth.

Fortunately Daniel kept most of the girls distracted. I had previously seen him as quiet and shy, but being surrounded by people (especially females) of his own age seemed to draw him out of his shell. He permanently had his arms round at least two of the girls, accompanying one to the lane each time it was her go and putting his arms around her waist to show her where to stand and how to bowl the ball. According to Daniel she still hadn't learned how to perform this by her twentieth go, and he insisted on 'helping' her for the rest of the night. There were the inevitable flickers of interest in my Englishness from the girls, and Daniel revelled in his newly discovered confidence to poke fun at me with the usual abuse – '*Inglese boiola*' (English gay) and all that.

We had to stay at the bowling alley for a while – well, we couldn't force Bruno to leave his new true love could we? The time was getting on though, and at 11.15pm, and with Bruno still only at the kissing stage with his new girl with braces, we rang a taxi to take us back. The taxi arrived at 11.59. Oswaldo would be locking the Casa dos Filtros doors at midnight. Bruno was still no further with his girl, and admitted defeat by accompanying us into the taxi. He had the girl's number, but he wanted so much more.

We told the taxi driver to '*vamos*', an instruction that he was only too happy to obey. The driver showed a similar disregard for red lights as Fabrice, though he did at least slow down slightly before going through them. We arrived at 12.07am to find the doors all locked. None of us really fancied the punishment of cleaning the toilets, so I embarked on my first journey through the window.

The wall was surprisingly easy to scale and even Vicente, whose arm was in a sling after suffering a broken elbow in training, managed to scramble over with no trouble. After that it was just a simple case of having to dive through my bedroom window. The whole operation took about a minute, and we successfully avoided being noticed by either Joaquim or Oswaldo. I had joined the ranks of the rule-breakers. And the toilets would have to remain uncleaned.

9
LOST IN TRANSLATION

My leg was shaking. Someone had a firm hold of it. 'Hey sleeping beauty, wake up man,' came the familiar voice with its unique American/Ali G accent. Yago was standing over my bunk bed. It was a surprise, he didn't usually turn up unannounced and I had not seen him since *Feijoada*.

'I can't stay long, man. I have to go soon. My car is outside, I am going home to Florianopolis, I have to do some school exams. I'm not coming back after Christmas.' I couldn't believe it. My Google translate was going. How would I communicate with everyone? And what about Tangrianne? When would I see her now?

Yago continued: 'Emerson, he does not want me to play in the Copa São Paulo. I go home to find a team in Florianopolis and study. I will miss you, man. You have my Facebook, we speak on that.' We high-fived and hugged and that was that. Yago sped off on the eight-hour drive to the airport in Cuiaba in his 4x4, this time with his 'crooked' uncle driving.

I felt sad. My best friend in the whole of the country had left my life just like that. True, I had survived the previous few weeks without him but I always thought he was coming back. I had no idea how long I was going to be in Brazil for.

Communication wasn't one of the Brazilians' greatest strengths – the Chairman could only speak a few English words, and in the last month he had told me I would sign professionally for SEC after the Copa São Paulo, that I'd sign for

Sinop – at 150km away, SEC's local rivals – after the Copa São Paulo, that there was a 'problem', even that I'd sign for a team in Switzerland. Anderson made it no clearer. He told me I'd be moving to São Paulo. Chandler had invited me to stay at his house in Rio Grande de Sul after the Copa São Paulo. So had Daniel Lucini. For all I knew I might well have ended up back in England.

Yago was the only person I could get any sense out of, my only means of ensuring the Chairman did nothing crazy and loaned me out to a team in Turkmenistan. For all of my worries though, I understood that I could well be in Brazil for months, if not years. I had just about managed the three weeks without my best friend and my main method of communication, but three years? And Tangrianne...

Then again, I had been in the country long enough to gain a conversational level of Brazilian Portuguese. I couldn't understand Emerson's long ramblings, but I picked up on the odd phrase, and could get by in basic conversations. There was only one person with whom I interacted now that could speak fluent English and I only saw him a couple of times a month.

Eduardo Vitali was Andrei's 16-year-old cousin, and his father, Elton, was a director of the football club. Elton was one of the keenest people to get me involved at the football club and one of my most ardent supporters, frequently pushing for me to get so much game time despite my lack of ability when compared to my team-mates. He had reason for his support though. Eduardo was trying to get in to Cambridge University, and his father had spotted an ideal way for him to improve his English.

And so it was that I was invited to the Vitali household every other week. Elton fed me pizza and let me play with their pet parrot. He knew that I detested the rice and beans served for every meal at Casa dos Filtros and so he bought me whatever food I desired and always made sure that I had an extra 50 Reais in the brown envelope containing my wages at the end of each month. All for just talking to his son for an hour or so. But Eduardo Vitali wasn't a realistic way for me to get any sense out of the Chairman. He wasn't going to be there at the training ground.

And how could I see Tangrianne? I hadn't seen her since *Feijoada* and now I had no link to her nor means of contacting her. The memory of her warm body was vivid, as was the smell of her perfume and the thought of her welcoming smile. Did I really want something to happen? It was Mum's worst nightmare that I would marry a Brazilian while out there.

Yago had been gone barely 10 minutes. I checked my phone, hoping in the back of my mind that Yago or, even better, Tangrianne would somehow flash up on my phone. Surely they hadn't left my life forever? The sun shone through the gap in the barred window, reflecting my face onto the screen of my iPhone. I stared for a few seconds. Nothing happened, nobody was trying to contact me. I stared for longer, this time looking at my face. It was an older face than that which had arrived a couple of months earlier.

The wispy bum fluff on my chin was beginning to turn to stubble. My skin, now less blemished with white pimples, was a healthy shade of orange. My mouth was curved slightly downward. I couldn't bear to look at my saddened lips. My eyes moved upward, toward my forehead. What was that line? What was that line?! I ran to the bathroom. There were a few Brazilians in there already. I forgot pleasantries for the more important task at hand. Cold water trickled out of the only working tap at the sink. I held out my welcoming hands before splashing it over my forehead. The line wouldn't wash off. I tried to straighten it out. No luck. It was permanent. My first forehead wrinkle had appeared at the tender age of 18.

Dismayed, I turned around to see an even worse sight. Michel was sat on one of the doorless toilets with a *Playboy* magazine in his hands, slowly rubbing his penis up and down at the sight of those glossy girls. Having caught my eye he gave me a thumbs-up and a cheery smile. At least he had the decency to attempt to find a partially hidden place to carry out the act – Fernando and Luciano were both masturbating in the communal showers. Roger was in between them, though he was embarking on the cultural practice of removing every single hair from his body.

'Hey, faggot', Roger greeted me, 'I shave you legs, OK?'

'No, no. I no gay', I replied.

'*Viado, Inglese*'.

I had long been ridiculed for my refusal to shave my legs. In Brazil it is believed that only homosexuals refrain from shaving their legs (though most homosexuals also shaved their legs). My team-mates did not believe me that the vast majority of English men do not shave their legs. I must be gay, they insisted. The facts added up for them: I was considered 'much bad' with the females, did not go crazy for the overweight females that Leo so loved and had not shaved every single hair on my body. None of my team-mates had hair anywhere except from on their head; not even their armpits. Whenever I headed to the bathroom there would usually be a naked Brazilian wandering around attempting to shave every hair off of his body.

And if there wasn't a naked Brazilian shaving there would almost certainly be a naked Brazilian pleasuring himself. The *Playboy* magazine that Michel was using lived in the bathroom. I think it had replaced the toilet brush, which had now virtually taken up a permanent residence on the dining table. It only ever got moved back to the toilet on the rare occasions that we were all forced into cleaning the house, and it would only ever last in its natural habitat for a couple of days at most.

My legs remained unshaved, but that bonus could not mask the devastating morning I had had thus far. Yago was gone. I'd never see Tangrianne again. I had a forehead wrinkle. I was no longer a boy. I jumped back on to my bed with all of the day's developments racing through my head. Which one was worst? My mind had been racing for an hour when Chandler headed over.

'Yago...leave', he said, forming a fist before releasing it to emphasise leaving, just in case his English was incorrect. 'Is much bad'. He put his hand on my shoulder with a concerned look on his face. 'Ah', he clicked his fingers as if he had just had a lightbulb moment. He reached over to his bed, grabbing his laptop. Google translate had already been loaded. Chandler began to type.

'Yago leaving must be hard for you. His cousin has left too, she has gone to school in Sinop. It is a shame. He was trying to get you to marry her. If you marry her, you can play for SEC forever. That is what we all wanted. We all wanted you to marry her. Now we have to find you a new girl. Yago was a good friend for you too. I can help you as much as Yago did.'

I was stunned. Tangrianne was gone. It had been a set-up all along, they had all been in on it, trying to get me to be with Tangrianne. I now understood why Yago had been beaming with pride. He was pleased with his own work. I understood why Yago's oldest cousin had punched that man at *Feijoada* for merely looking at Tangrianne. But now it didn't matter. She was gone.

It meant a lot that my team-mates wanted me to play for SEC and stay in Brazil. But it couldn't hide the fact that my best friend was gone, along with his cousin whom I had shared so many close moments with. Chandler spoke to me via Google translate for over an hour until we were disturbed by lunch.

There was no session that afternoon, and I continued to mull things over on my bed until dinner. I felt quite sombre, my mood sad. But there was no point in getting too hung up. A Brazilian Christmas was just two days away and I was fascinated by what it would be like.

10
CHRISTMAS AT THE CASA

Casa dos Filtros was only half full on Christmas Eve. Those who were rich enough, about 10 of them, flew home to spend the holiday with their families. The rest of us were left to mill around the house. Christmas Eve is a special time in Brazil, reflected in our generous portions of rice and beans for dinner. Not only were we allowed two pieces of salty beef each, but chips were also on the menu.

Despite not being with their loved ones, the Brazilians were all brimming with excitement, jabbering about attending church that evening. Admittedly I found it a bit harder to get excited – it just didn't seem right to be celebrating Christmas in 40-degree heat. I was intrigued about attending church that evening, though. From what I had seen with my team-mates, I was sure that it was going to be a spectacle.

It certainly was. Bizarrely given the weather, the centre of Sorriso was decorated as a winter wonderland. There were stalls, some depicting the birth of Christ but most posing as Father Christmas's workshop, and Christmas lights mainly in the shape of snow flakes. Plastic reindeer and Santas abound-ed, set among red and white canes sticking out of the ground. There was a lot of fake snow. Sorriso, I was told, had never seen the real stuff. A few of my team-mates from the South, such as Daniel Lucini from Rio Grande de Sul, told me they had on occasions.

The Brazilian players went to different churches and once in the city, five or six of them veered off. I stuck with Rian, Dudu and the fourth-choice goalkeeper, Tangerina (who couldn't understand why I called him Laranja, which means orange) and headed for their place of worship.

It seemed that many others had the same idea, and when we turned the corner, we were greeted by a silent sea of Brazilians, punctuated only by a large white cross, nearly as high as the church itself, which had *Messoes Populares e Hora de Evangeliza 2002* printed on it. The building, the Evangelical church, was bright blue and not far off the size of the football stadium. Despite this, it was so overcrowded that it was impossible to get inside, and hordes of people surrounded each window.

There came a collective groan as a third camera crew rushed in through the main doors, displacing another 20 onlookers. The service wasn't even due to start for another 10 minutes. After a quick walk around the church perimeter we worked out that there was zero chance of us getting inside, and almost no chance of getting a view of the service through the window. Rian took the lead, deciding that we should get in the queue at the main entrance and wait for people to leave. But nobody was going to.

And so we barged in, our main weapon Rian himself, who cut a sizeable figure and was adept at pushing people out of the way. Our aggressive manner could not have contrasted more with the scene inside. Everywhere people were hugging, couples and families, and friends weeping, all silently watching the proceedings at the front of the church.

'Sefi!' Rian cried before giving me a kiss that I did not return. I didn't have a clue what the priest was saying, nor any of the children invited to speak, but it was obviously very moving and prompting all the emotion in the building. For Dudu it was too much. Tears streamed down his face as he fingered his cross. Tangerina kept on crossing himself.

I was glad when we finally decided to go. As amazing as the scene that greeted me inside the church was, the novelty wore off after 15 minutes or so, my amazement replaced with indifference and finally boredom. We left before the end of the service. Rian decided that we had paid enough respect and spent the next five minutes helping us barge back out of the church through the sea of Brazilians. Our vacated spaces were snapped up within seconds. Outside the crowds had thinned. There were now only a few people around the windows. Most had probably retreated to their homes to watch the proceedings on television. They certainly hadn't gone elsewhere. We saw nobody on the walk back to Casa dos Filtros.

The Chairman greeted us there with a large cake, decorated as a football pitch with 'SEC' written on it. After watching us dig in he called me over. 'Sefi…this, my, errrrr, girlfriend'. He nodded to the girl on his left. She smiled. She was stunning. Long black hair flowed down her curvy figure. Her eyes sparkled. She couldn't have been much older than me, maybe a few years. She could quite easily be mistaken for the Chairman's daughter. Perhaps the Chairman had got his English mixed up, which he frequently did.

'*Ola*' I said in my best Portuguese accent, shaking the girl's hand. I didn't want to go for the continental style kiss on each cheek; who knew how the Chairman would react? A handshake was safe. The Chairman laughed before inviting me to a festival with his girlfriend and Joaquim. I had planned to go to a party in the city with a few of my team-mates that evening, but knowing that the Chairman had a large say on whether I signed as a professional, I accepted. I had to keep him happy and on my side. I only had to cast my mind back to the Three Street fiasco, not to mention the many altercations with the bus drivers, to realise that I certainly did not want to make the Chairman angry.

The Chairman was very pleased that I accepted. He gave his girlfriend a big kiss to show that his English had in fact been correct and that she was actually his girlfriend. He summoned Joaquim straight away, and insisted that we must leave immediately. I didn't even have a chance to say goodbye to anyone. When the Chairman insisted you did something you did it.

He was very excited. He had his arm around his girlfriend whilst driving and was enjoying the raucous laughs he received from Joaquim when telling him of how I was a '*boiola*' and the spitting image of Elton John.

'Sing, Elton John, sing'. They roared at me.

'*Foda-se*' I replied, to great roars of approval. Even the Chairman's girlfriend, not offended by an Englishman saying 'Fuck you', gave me a smile.

'Much good Sefi, much good. Next, errrr, *anos*. You. Professional... here. Sorriso.'

His eyes lit up as he got to the end of the sentence. He was obviously very proud that he had completed a sentence in English, and his girlfriend beamed at the intellectual excellence of her man. 'But... errrr.... but.... Anderson. Problem. Complication!' He spat out the word in disgust before assuring me: 'Sefi, professional. I Sefi, professional. Congratulations.' I nodded and smiled as I was sure I was expected to, and the Chairman continued with his good spirits. 'Excellent Sefi!'

To my pleasant surprise, the Chairman's rusted Fiat Punto pulled into Andrei's farm. Throughout the journey I had been concerned about the 'festival', so it was reassuring to see a familiar face upon arrival. The Chairman greeted Andrei's father like he was a brother, and they shared an emotional hug which lasted for a long time. Following this, the Chairman presented his stunning girlfriend, giving her a kiss to prove that she was his girlfriend and his alone. He treated her as if she were his property.

The 'festival' turned out to be a party for all of Andrei's family at his house, with a few especially invited guests. Music played and some people were dancing. The rest milled about, talking and laughing. The Chairman headed straight for the alcohol, pouring himself and Andrei's father two large glasses. Whereas Andrei was slim and streamlined, his father was overweight and balding with glasses. I presumed that it was because of his weight that he had a rather pink complexion and breathed heavily. His personality was not unlike Joaquim's, always jolly and roaring with laughter. He was a stereotypical chef, and he had served up quite a feast for the evening festivities. His finest animals had been cooked up for the benefit of his hungry guests, and they were part of a mouth-watering spread. The spread was not to be touched until the clock struck midnight. First we had to celebrate together.

After being entertained by a man with a guitar, we were led in song by Andrei's father, who had a drunk Chairman swaying on his right shoulder. Then, 15 minutes before midnight, we all congregated into a circle, held hands and sang soft hymns together. Andrei's father roared as midnight struck, and we all set about hugging each other before tucking into the spread.

Getting drunker and drunker, the Chairman was wandering around the farm with a contented look on his face, occasionally bursting into fits of giggles. His girlfriend, who hadn't drunk all night (was she even old enough to drink?), wore a concerned look, but her attempts to make sure the Chairman was OK were merely batted away. Whatever he was drinking, Andrei's father must also have been on. Just one hour after midnight Andrei's father was fast asleep under the spread, his complexion even pinker and blotchier than before. My conversation with Andrei was being interrupted by loud snores. Andrei looked over lovingly. 'My dad, he crazy man,' he said.

Suddenly the Chairman appeared out of nowhere. He

pointed at Andrei's father and giggled, before declaring that he was going off in his car and would be back in 30 minutes. His girlfriend, who had tamed him to the extent that he no longer shook her off, would accompany him. The Chairman wobbled toward his rusted Punto, and, after some prompts from his girlfriend, managed to open the driver's door. A further 30 seconds passed as he attempted to get the keys in the ignition. The Punto then spluttered into life as the Chairman slowly guided the car into the distance.

He never returned to the party. I'd lost Joaquim too. Eventually, I returned to Casa dos Filtros at 3am, after Andrei drove me back across town in his father's pick-up truck. I returned to a silent house with all of its doors locked. It was a bit late to be tackling the window, but my brain informed my tired body that this was the only route to bed. Once through, I discovered an empty house. Everyone was still obviously out partying.

I was only allowed three hours of sleep as everyone returned from their revelling at 6.30am. They didn't have to go through the window this time – Chandler had the front door key. But rather than head straight for their beds, they got a football out and had a kickabout. Chandler was soon taking charge and arranged a keepie-uppie tournament to be played in three of the rooms. Inebriation and sleep-deprivation teamed up against the Brazilians, allowing me to enjoy a quite comfortable victory. Finally, at 8am, just when we'd usually be concluding breakfast prior to training, it was decided that we should probably get some sleep.

It felt strange having no authority figures in the house. Oswaldo was back home in Belem and who knew where Joaquim had ended up. Without our wake-up call we slept until 2pm. Viniscius and Michel still hadn't returned. In Sorriso – and in the rest of Brazil, I gathered – Christmas Eve was for family and Christmas Day for friends. Because of this, it had been arranged for us to spend the afternoon at Clube Piscina.

Unfortunately whoever organised the trip was not great at counting, as a shortage of taxis meant that eight of us were left behind. When more taxis finally arrived and we made it to Clube Piscina, I was disappointed. I had hoped for another rainforest adventure, but was greeted by a commercial adventure park. Home felt a long way away. The Christmas Day lunch of rice, beans and salty beef hadn't helped, but now I really wanted to see my family. A phone call to them had not really done much to lift some homesickness I was feeling.

I shouldn't have felt like this. Clube Piscina had more than enough to keep me entertained. A large swimming pool was its centrepiece, and there were all sorts of slides built around it. Next to this was a dance floor and bar area. Then there were large grassy areas, cafes and beach volleyball courts. The whole park was packed. After paying five Reais for entry we headed straight for these beach volleyball courts, where we found some of our team playing *futvolley*.

Foolishly I tried to join them but didn't even get both feet on to the court. A sharp pain went through my foot as I stepped on the burning hot sand. My team-mates laughed at my yelp and jump into the air as they showed me that I had to use the hose to soak the sand with water before stepping on it. Even then, it was hard to stand still for more than a few seconds. When the ball went out of play, it meant a comical scene of a number of Brazilians hopping from foot to foot.

Futvolley is one of Brazil's favourite games. Essentially it is beach volleyball, except that players may use any part of their body apart from the hands. My inexperience told as I failed to control ball after ball. Defeated, and with burning feet, I accompanied a group to the swimming pool. We were disappointed, though. We had only gone to the swimming pool to stare at the women in their bikinis, something made easier under the disguise of sunglasses, but it was soon declared that all of the women were too fat, even for Leo. Bruno still managed to kiss one.

After a lengthy kickabout in the grass park we decided that it was just about time to go. Once again I had to wait an eternity for a taxi. When I finally got back to Casa dos Filtros, I was met with the leftovers from lunch. Viniscius and Michel still weren't back. I was homesick but there would not be time to wallow in it for too long.

11
NAME CALLING (1)

We were brought back to Earth with a bang on Boxing Day as Emerson attempted to run all the Christmas festivities out of us with an intense double session. It was all a bit too much for Viniscius and Michel, who had clambered back through the window, still drunk and full of festivity, while the rest of the team were at breakfast. They surprisingly managed to make the morning session, but training in the afternoon was just a bridge too far for them and they decided to sleep through the afternoon instead. They were still both asleep when we finished dinner that evening.

The Chairman turned up toward the end of dinner with a belated Christmas present for Casa dos Filtros: a table tennis table. A tournament was set up within minutes, and it immediately looked like the table was going to play a big part in our lives. The Chairman left happy, satisfied with his work, though not before telling me that I was going to sign for the Sorriso senior team after the Copa São Paulo. As had become common practice with the Chairman, I smiled and nodded my head but knew not to believe him until I had signed something.

The sound of an unhealthy Fiat Punto coughing into motion had hardly left Casa dos Filtros when disaster struck. For some reason the Chairman had deemed one ping pong ball enough to last us. He hadn't accounted for Luciano's size 12s coming down on the thing. The crunch brought a silence. Luciano looked to his left, then his right, then stopped.

He dashed into his room, and came back minutes later clasping his roll-on deodorant. With 20 pairs of intrigued eyes watching him, he proceeded to the kitchen where he found a large knife, which he used to cut the roll-on ball from the package. Triumphantly he smiled, throwing the unwashed ball towards Rian. I was sure I saw an armpit hair on it and made a mental note to wait a while before touching it, personal hygiene having become a much more pressing issue after the soap incident. Nobody cared too much though; Luciano had saved the day. The new ball wasn't quite the same – it moved much more quickly and was a greater test of reactions – but it did the basic job of a ball.

For the Brazilians, the entertainment of playing ping pong all evening was beaten the next evening at the internet cafe. I had been encouraged to sign up to Orkut – a social media website popular in Brazil – and finally gave in to the demands. The laughter started when Chandler saw the profile I created.

'Look, his name! Sefi BOQUET! Oh my God! Oh my God!' The disbelieving Brazilians swarmed around the screen. They all agreed that my name was hilarious. 'No, no', I tried to correct them, 'Seth BURKETT, not BOQUET', but it was too late.

Luciano at least tried to follow my pronunciation: 'Jeff Boquet?' he questioned. It had become plain that I was never, ever, going to be allowed to live this down. '*Boquet*' translated as 'blowjob', with '*boqueteiro*', which had now become another nickname, meaning 'cocksucker'.

So here I was, Seth Blowjob, or Seth Cocksucker depending on who you were speaking to, a name which was confirmed by my refusal to shave my legs. Delighted with their work, the Brazilians set about interrogating me on the rest of my family's names. My Dad and sister were deemed to have disappointing names, but it was my Mum who truly set them off.

I thought that Viniscius was having a fit, so frantic was his laughter. 'Clare' apparently translated as 'thrust', and Leo and Michel wasted no time in creating a little song and dance, chanting 'And Clare, and Boquet,' repeatedly. There was no respite even when we left the internet cafe. As soon as we stepped in the front door of Casa dos Filtros, all those not at the cafe were quickly informed of the new discovery, which had the same comedic effect. Sounds of 'and Clare, and Boquet' rang through the house for the rest of the night.

I was glad for that day to end but took comfort from a sense that the Brazilians, naturally good-natured, were not laughing AT me – although, yes, they were laughing at my expense – but WITH me. In that was the difference between the team bonding in Brazil and the classic macho world of 'dressing room banter' in England. Out here, it was very much a team; they laughed at me because they knew that I could take it and would give some back. On reflection, the whole episode actually brought me closer to my team-mates – it was another thing that we could bond over and laugh about.

In Brazil no man is an island. In England, I felt that every man was a planet, hopelessly isolated and forced to fight for just himself. It is not always the case, and there are some genuinely nice people in the game in England, but there almost seems to be a dynamic to dressing rooms that is handed down. The 'banter' that flies about is often shameless bullying, and the chief protagonist usually asserts himself by relentlessly pointing out the flaws in the weak link of the team – usually the worst player, the youngster, or the new, unproven member of the squad. The weak link then learns that this is how to assert oneself within a football team, and goes about reproducing the behaviour that he witnesses.

The joshing in Brazil was never personal. Yes, they had laughed at my surname, but if a Brazilian came over to

England with the name Ronaldo Blowjob I'm sure he would get the mickey taken out of him. Yes, they had called me a monster when I erupted in spots after essentially washing with their sweaty boxers, but this had never been malicious, and always done with a smile.

In England I barely went a week without being reminded that I had a big nose, or a 'beak'. One player called me greaseball. I'd hate to think of the names I was called out of earshot. As with Brazil, these names were always said with a smile, though unlike Brazil these smiles seemed false, the aim of the protagonist being to assert himself further within the social nucleus of the team without thought for the recipient. Here at Sorriso, there were no cliques – everybody socialised with everybody, everybody got on with everybody, everybody laughed with everybody. Even Viniscius. I agreed with Cassius that Brazil was a warm place.

* * *

I was getting used to the morning routine: awoken with a harsh shake and ordered to get my kit. The Copa São Paulo was looming and training had taken on an added intensity since the Christmas break. There was still time for laughter, for breaking into spontaneous dance and playing music, but as soon as we got on to the training field things got serious. Even Leo listened attentively to Emerson's daily pre-training speech.

If the sessions themselves had stepped up a level, then so had the media interest, and it was usual for there to be a representative from the radio, another from a newspaper and at least one television crew at each session. And at each session they wanted me. The football world may be infatuated with Brazil, but equally Brazil has a love for English football. The spiritual home of the game still recognised the ancestral home, the nation from which the great sport grew, and the nation which introduced them to the beautiful game.

For the media, and as my story even widened occasionally to the rest of Brazil, I represented the home of football. I was England, and the fact that I had come to learn from them was both fascinating and a compliment of the highest regard. By now I could even say a couple of words in Portuguese when interviewed, though these usually only extended as far as 'here much hot', meaning that a translator was still necessary. Fortunately the interviewer would always refer to me as 'Borkett' rather than 'Boquet', thus sparing my dignity.

Our final session in Sorriso before the Copa São Paulo, conducted on the morning of New Year's Eve, was especially for the press. We were given our official kit for the tournament (including a horrific shiny blue nylon shell suit with the Sorriso crest, which looked like it came straight out of the 1960s) and then had to pose for numerous photographs. The coaches then did their interviews for another half an hour while we were told to play *Rondos* or do kick-ups for the video cameras.

Finally we were allowed to start the session, which was a fun two-touch match. Quite a crowd had gathered to see us off, and they sat fanning themselves in the small area of shade that the stadium roof provided. Some school children were jumping at the fence, eager to shout their best wishes. The support was truly flattering, and it was easy to see why.

There was a great sense of community in Sorriso. The football stadium remained unlocked at all times. More often than not, we would arrive to afternoon training to the sight of masses of school children, some barefoot, joyfully dribbling a ball through the bare patches of turf and pretending to be their favourite footballer.

The surrounding athletics track was also used frequently by both schools and the local athletics club. The stadium was a real community hub, and right at the centre of this hub was Sorriso Esporte Clube.

As I had seen at Vitoria, the team recognised their position, and the respect that they had for their supporters was evident: that sign *Obrigado por prestigar o esporte* – thank you for honouring the sport – was painted in large, bright red letters on the commentary box located above the main stadium entrance. This respect is mutual, and turns into adoration on match days or special occasions such as this. I think my performance entertained the onlookers. I got an assist, scored an own goal, got nutmegged by Fabrice (who seemed to have gained at least a stone over Christmas), was crunched by Fernando and eventually forced off the pitch after receiving a split lip courtesy of Andrei's elbow.

We were given the afternoon off to give us time to pack our bags. I had earlier been dismayed to learn that we would not be flying to São Paulo, but would instead be travelling the 1,200 miles by bus. That is the equivalent of driving from London to Budapest - except that London to Budapest would largely be done on smooth, tarmac roads. The vast majority of roads that I had travelled on from Cuiaba had been dirt tracks regularly punctuated by pot holes.

Even worse was that we were scheduled to leave at 6am on New Year's Day. This didn't deter my teammates (they were Brazilian after all so how could they turn down a party?), and the majority headed off into the city that evening, first making sure that the window with the missing bar was left firmly open. On reflection I should have joined them, but the lure of the large good luck cake in the kitchen and an early night proved too much. Instead I joined Leandro and Fernando in hitting the ball of Luciano's armpit sweat around the ping pong table.

Leandro, although not suffering the same crippling poverty as Fernando, also originated from the Rio de Janeiro favelas.

After playing table tennis for an hour or so, the three of us retreated to the seating area, and I felt that it was a good moment to get to know Leandro better. He was quite a slight individual, with short curly hair and a large, toothy smile. He had definitely never benefited from braces. A star was tattooed over each of his elbows – the left star had *mae* (mother) inscribed in it, the right had *pae* (father).

Leandro was one of the most religious people in the team. His full name, Leandro Jesus de Silva, was testament to this, and he wore his cross around his neck with immense pride. His smile was almost as permanent a fixture as the two stars on his elbows, and he had every reason to be happy. He was getting paid to do something that he loved. As with Fernando he would send a percentage of his monthly wages in an envelope back to his family home, though this would never amount to more than 100 Reais.

Leandro's family, though suffering from poverty, were not in as desperate a situation as Fernando's. Still, the pride that Leandro felt from helping his family was obvious, and the 200 Reais he kept each month equated to fantastic riches. I was sure that the financial benefits of football would last far beyond the Copa São Paulo for Leandro. He was an exceptional footballer, and truly played with a spontaneous freedom that comes from a feeling of pure joy whilst doing something you love. Technically he was superb, and he excelled in the advanced midfield position in which he played. Whereas most players flitted between Emerson's first and second choices, Leandro was in the holy club consisting of Viniscius, Chandler, Luis and Andrei who were deemed irreplaceable.

'In Rio, there is much bang bang', Leandro said, miming guns with his hands. 'As well, there are drugs, much drugs'. Fernando nodded. 'I cannot leave my house at night'. He reached for a flip flop. 'This, my house'. He pointed at the flip flop. He pointed to the sides of the flip flop, representing the three streets surrounding his house. It emerged that each of these streets was occupied by a different drug gang, none of whom was too friendly towards each other.

The disguise of darkness made it impossible to be safe at night, he continued. Pickpockets were rife. Even in the day Leandro had to be alert and cautious at all times. The drug gangs ran the streets. The pickpockets were the rats, and were often encouraged by the drug gangs, as whatever they were able to steal went toward funding their drug habit. The police would occasionally intervene, but were too scared – or sensible – to have a constant presence. When they did intervene, Leandro told me how his family would have to cross their fingers and hope for the best. Several times the police had burst into their house. Once they had shot some rubber bullets. Often they opened random fire (this is what I guessed from Leandro's wild gesticulations) across the favela with their rubber bullets. Fernando had it even worse; at least Leandro did not have sewage running through his street.

No wonder both of them were so happy in Sorriso, which provided them with a lifestyle that was beyond their wildest dreams. And no wonder so many young men in Brazil looked to football for an escape into a different way of life.

12
UP FOR THE COPA...

An overnight bus journey lasting a full day and a half: what a way to start the New Year. In true Brazilian style we set off for São Paulo two hours after the scheduled time of 6am and I could see the disappointment in my team-mates who had returned through the window at 3am. They could have enjoyed another two hours of partying.

We were greeted by a brand new double decker bus complete with televisions, air conditioning and a toilet. What a treat and relief after the bus we had used thus far, which I doubted would be able to take us much out of Sorriso, let alone the 1,200 miles to São Paulo. Now we had two bus drivers, who would change over every time we stopped for food. There seemed to be an endless supply of them in Sorriso, the Chairman having sacked more than I could count. I wondered whether these ones were aware of what they had let themselves in for. They were just as likely to be sacked in São Paulo and their bus seized from them, leaving them stranded.

A small gathering of people had come to see us off. Though the majority seemed to be suits from the club, it was also refreshing to see a few locals offering their support. Once again we had to spend an extravagant amount of time posing for all kinds of photographs. We were joined on the bus by Fabrice, who was organising our schedule while we were in São Paulo.

Although Fabrice was a great character I was unsure how sensible it was to appoint a man who still laughed at fart jokes as the leader of our squad, which had now been whittled to 28, with five not making the final cut. As well as Yago having departed, midfield players Lucas and Charles had gone, along with defenders Andre and Charles.

The latter Charles was also a left back and so much did I improve over my first few weeks in Sorriso that Emerson released him. As much as I liked him, I had been ecstatic as it showed I was cementing my place in the squad. My attitude had been changed, I guess, by something that happened to me when I was a teenager at Peterborough and I had become a little more individualistic about the game.

A coach had asked me if I wanted a certain player in our squad to get a scholarship. I replied that I did. It prompted a tirade from him. 'Don't give a fuck about him. Just care about your fucking self,' he told me. 'Does he care if you get a scholarship? Does he fuck. All you should care about it making it yourself. It's a competition. You can't all get contracts. You have to be the fucking best.'

Anyway, Fabrice got on the bus and reminded me how he had nutmegged me before positioning himself on the lower deck with the the coaching staff and a few suits. The Chairman would not be attending, much to the bus drivers' delight, as he had decided that he was needed in Sorriso to deal with the professional side who were now back in preparation for their own season in the senior Campeonato Matogrossense.

All the players headed up to the upper deck and most went straight to sleep. They weren't missing much – the view from the window amounted to nothing more than miles and miles of soya bean fields. Every now and again we would travel over a deep pothole, and the subsequent lurch would awaken the group, but other than that the bus was quiet until lunchtime.

The new bus may have been an improvement on the old one, but it proved to be no more reliable by breaking down immediately after a quick lunch of pizza. We were left waiting for over an hour while it was fixed. Leonardo had brought a ukulele and kept us entertained. Once on the move again, Dudu made himself a drum and joined Leonardo in song, prompting a few of the team to samba up and down the aisle.

Leo also performed his party piece – a Michael Jackson moonwalk impression. The star seemed to be known as Mike Jacks in Brazil and had become revered in the country since his death. At Casa dos Filtros, Leo had found a videotape of his greatest hits and it was often left playing on repeat on the TV in the communal area. Every night, Leo would honour his hero with a moonwalk before grabbing his crotch and screaming 'Oww!'.

By now the soya bean fields had been replaced by continuous forest with the odd shack. The roads were still little more than dusty tracks, which meant that we were unable to go much faster than 30mph. After 12 hours we finally made it out of the state of Mato Grosso. I couldn't get over Brazil's enormity. We slept overnight on the bus.

As we approached São Paulo the land became more urbanised. Not only were the roads now tarmac, but we were also treated to travelling on dual carriageway, leading to gleeful cries of *'vamos motorista'*. At 8pm, and just over 36 hours since leaving Sorriso, we pulled into the Terraco Perea hotel in the town of São Carlos. We were still 250 kilometres away from the city of São Paulo, but we were informed that this was where we were to be based for our group games.

The hotel was a welcome break from Casa dos Filtros, not least because the toilet brush was in its correct place and there was a bathroom door to protect one's dignity. The rooms were smart and whitewashed, and offered so much more space than the cramped conditions back in Sorriso, but the most pleasing feature of our room for four was a television with channels that

showed English football. I had never been more thrilled to witness such a low-key affair as Reading versus Liverpool.

Fabrice had chosen the rooms, and I was put in with Lucas
Castanhol, a midfield player, Luciano and Leonardo (who had
taken to my nickname of 'Di Caprio' to avoid any confusion
with Leo and now everyone had to refer to him as Di Caprio).
Luciano and Leonardo were both centre halves and potentially
menacing but they were both joyful individuals. Leonardo
was always dancing and playing his music and Luciano always
laughing.

Lucas Castanhol was quiet, and kept himself to himself.
He was from the North of Brazil, right in the depths of the
Amazon rainforest. Although the North is known to be poorer
than the South, I presumed that he was quite well-off as he was
one of the lucky ones who had gone home for Christmas and
now his parents had flown into town to watch their son play in
the Copa São Paulo.

Lucas and Leonardo were both good room-mates, though
I did have a concern with Luciano. I got on really well with
him, as he didn't have a bad bone in his body and he made me
laugh, but he could be irritating. Since the day he arrived he had
been in love with my iPhone, especially with one of the driving
games on it. He always greeted me with the phrase 'Play game?',
a request which had come nearly hourly on the long bus journey. I had become so frustrated with his limited vocabulary
back in Casa dos Filtros that I attempted to teach him some
English. He came back the next day and proudly exclaimed,
'Hello, my name is cellular'. I realised that I was fighting a losing
battle after that.

We weren't alone in the hotel. Rio Branco and Palmeiras,
two of the other teams in our group, were also here. The Rio
Branco players had travelled even further than us – from 3,500
kilometres West – though they had sensibly decided to fly

instead of drive. They were all friendly, and seemed just as thrilled as us to be there.

The Palmeiras players, representing one of Brazil's mightiest clubs, national champions many times, from São Paolo itself, were at the other end of the spectrum. They weren't allowed to hang around in the lobby with either of the teams and were forbidden, indeed, to talk to anyone not wearing a Palmeiras tracksuit. Was there some kind of football class war going on? Did the Palmeiras coaches think that by talking to us their play-ers, representing a club whose seniors had been World Club Champions, would suddenly sink to our level of ability? They rarely even ate at the same time as us, and, to top it off, were banned from using the stairs. Walking up and down stairs used energy which could otherwise be used for football purposes. If you played for Palmeiras you had to use the elevator.

There were other guests in the hotel, among them a German swimming team, who also ate with us. My team-mates seemed outraged that I did not know them. The Germans were all even whiter than me, and because of their whiteness, the Brazilians decided that surely I must know them. They even referred to the Germans as '*Sefi's familia*'.

When the Germans finally left the dining area the attention turned away from me and my 'family', I used the time to look out from the balcony area at my new temporary home. São Carlos was like most Brazilian cities I had seen in geography lessons. High rise buildings in the centre, rich whitewashed houses with terracotta roofs surrounding them and smaller houses on the outskirts. I couldn't see any favelas or slums. They must have been obscured by the sea of green which met my eyes. Where there was no building there were trees every-where. It was calm, clean and even serene. This would be the closest we would get to the teeming city of São Paulo itself, the largest city in Brazil, and indeed the Southern Hemisphere, with its population of 11.5 million.

Our first training was scheduled for the afternoon of our first full day. Anderson arrived at the Terraco Perea just before lunch. The Copa was a great excuse for him to fly over to visit his family in São Paulo whilst checking up on me. I was grateful to see him – I owed him so much. The Brazilians were even more grateful to see him. It seemed like Viniscius was man-marking me over lunch. Now that Anderson was here I was Viniscius's best friend in the whole world. His logic was that if Anderson thought I was friendly with him, then Anderson would take a greater liking to Viniscius. And that meant that Anderson would grant Viniscius his dream of playing football in Europe.

For my team-mates, Anderson represented hope. They all dreamed of playing in Europe. Yes, they all agreed that the Brazilian league was the best in the world, that the Brazilian Ronaldo was, despite his spare tyre, still the best player in the world and that all their loved ones were in Brazil. But Europe was where the money was. If they played in Europe they would almost certainly return home rich beyond their wildest dreams. And then think what they could buy their loved ones – Fernando could buy his family a home, maybe even a car, Luciano could finally buy his own iPhone, Viniscius could boast to his friends. Such was their view of Europe that the fact that I had played there meant I deserved respect on the field.

The pitch that greeted us for training was even worse than ours in Sorriso. The wispy grass came up to just under our knees across the whole pitch, with not even one bare patch of turf. I feared that we might lose poor little Daniel in the grass. Emerson recognised that a full session in such conditions would be problematic, so he based the session on recovery after that long journey.

We slowly jogged around a lot, stretched even more, and

then walked around for a bit while the television cameras got their pictures. I was pulled aside for an interview along with Emerson and Luis. When the camera crew had finally finished, Emerson allowed us a fun two-touch match. It had to be two-touch really, with dribbling impossible. He later complained to the organisers and the grass was cut for our next session, but not before we had to endure a session on another, waterlogged, pitch where Leandro's weaving dribbles saw him leave the ball behind, much to our amusement.

Anderson's girlfriend watched our first session, and she asked me how I found it as I headed for the bus back to the hotel. I told her that it was much easier as the weather here was a fair bit cooler than in Sorriso. It was 32 degrees, she said.

The Copa São Paulo was kicking off that afternoon, and we returned to the hotel to find it being screened in the reception area. The media interest in the tournament was incredible. I was overwhelmed by our relationship with the media in Sorriso, but somehow that had now intensified. SporTV – the most watched sports channel in Brazil – was pretty much giving the tournament 24/7 coverage. ESPN were also showing plenty. Most of the channels were showing highlights, including Globo – the second largest television network in annual revenue worldwide.

Over on SporTV, Corinthians of São Paulo were beating Rondonopolis 6-0 in front of a frenzied capacity crowd. It has been estimated that nearly 15% of Brazilians – some 30 million – support Corinthians and there is always a scramble for tickets to watch any team wearing the sacred club badge. The lucky few who manage to get tickets support the team with as much passion as if they were supporting the national team in a World Cup final.

It didn't matter that Rondonopolis proved to be no competition. The fans were still ecstatic that their boys had overcome the opposition. They were jumping up and down, screaming and letting off flares even after the final whistle. The 11 idols on the pitch saluted the sea of white before the cameras headed back to the studio. The post-match highlights and analysis ensued, before the analysts sat back to discuss the tournament.

My ears pricked up at the mention of '*Sefi, Inglese*'. My team-mates all roared approvingly. '*Inglese! Inglese!*' chanted Leo. The men were talking too fast for me to understand fully. By now I had acquired a reasonable command of Portuguese, but only if the other person spoke very slowly. And so it was that I was able to understand phrases such as 'plays left defence', 'played in the English eighth division for Stamford FC', 'coach Emerson Mattheus says...', but not much else. I think it was good, though, as my team-mates all seemed to approve.

I was soon to realise that this was not an isolated piece of coverage. The Brazilians were genuinely excited to see an English boy compete against the best players in their nation, and I was the talk of a number of chat shows. I awoke the morning of our first game, against the hosts, São Carlos, to see the manager of their team in the studios of Globo TV discussing me. After breakfast a camera crew came into my room. They said nothing, just pointed a camera at me and filmed me reading. Two minutes later, and without a word, they left. After lunch my *siesta* was disrupted when I awoke bleary eyed to see a video camera pointing at me. I had no idea how long they had been there.

Our game was not due to kick-off until 7pm but Emerson confined us to our rooms all day. We weren't even allowed to sit in the reception area. I learnt the hard way. After finishing my reading in the morning I headed to the lone computer in the reception to try and use the internet. I wasn't even able to sit down before Emerson bellowed 'Sefi', and gestured for me to get back upstairs. I've never moved so fast in my life.

Most of my team-mates spent all day sleeping. Those who didn't read their Bibles. They certainly came out in force, along with the crosses, at 5.30pm when we left the Terraco Perea for the game. The mood on the bus was serious. Leonardo had left his ukulele in the hotel room and there was no samba-ing down the aisles. Only a few stirred when an attractive woman walked past the bus. I'd never been on such a quiet bus in Brazil. The only sound that accompanied the faint folk music coming from Viniscius's netbook was the quiet murmur of Brazilians muttering prayers and reading scriptures.

The wealth inequality which was so obvious in Sorriso was less evident here in São Carlos. There were no clusters of huts with corrugated iron roofs. Advertising boards showed a quote from the Brazilian Prime Minister: 'São Carlos is an example for the whole of Brazil'. These boards appeared down nearly every street. Boards advertising the Copa São Paulo appeared down every other street. The logo of the tournament was set against a yellow and green background, with the games listed in bold. As we got closer to the ground there were more and more boards.

There was a growing buzz amongst the Brazilians. The streets were suddenly full of people, all clutching tickets. There were stalls selling São Carlos merchandise and police in riot gear. The overwhelming majority of people were wearing Palmeiras shirts (Palmeiras were playing Rio Branco after our game), though I was buoyed to spot two people wearing England shirts. A police car weaved in front of our bus, and safely led us to an entrance to the ground.

Oswaldo quickly got to work with laying out the kit and distributing boots while we went to inspect the pitch. The ground was modern, in a bowl shape. Blue and orange stands surrounded 75% of the pitch, the other 25% was open. The stand on the nearest touchline was raised, and had 5,000 covered seats, as

well as a large gantry. There were a number of cameras already
set up. The other stands had no seats, but the bright orange
blocks of terracing had room for 10,000 people. A wired fence
prevented spectators from invading the pitch. Some Palmeiras
supporters were clearly already in the ground, as this fence was
adorned with their banners. The pitch was not like any I had
seen since being in Brazil. There were no bare patches. None
of the grass came up to my knees. It was like a large green car-
pet, lovingly tended to produce a superb playing surface.

We had a setback just 45 minutes before the game. Dudu
and Leonardo's registrations had both failed, meaning that they
were ineligible. I was coming to know the Chairman and his
attitude to paperwork, so I was not surprised. None of this
was much use to me, however, as neither Dudu nor Leonardo
played in the left back position I so coveted.

Instead, Furlan was given the sacred number 6 shirt and
I had to settle for the substitute's bench. I liked Furlan. He
had a heart of gold, which made it easier for me to accept. He
brought me coconut water and chocolate cake from his mother.
Delighted that I was to have had my talent vindicated enough
to see off Charles's challenge for the left-back slot, perhaps
my liking for Furlan meant that I wasn't ruthless enough, as
that old Peterborough coach had suggested when I wanted a
colleague to get a scholarship. Then again, we were all in this
together. Besides, I might get on as a sub. And there were two
more group games after this one.

Leonardo had only been picked for the bench, so Daniel
received a late call to take his place. The failure of Dudu's
registration was more problematic, as he had been due to start
in an attacking midfield role. He was a classic Brazilian player who loved to run at defenders and was always full of joy.
Despite his age of just 16, Emerson held him in high regard.
Pelezinho took his place, with the other 13-year-old in our

squad, Leozinho, among the substitutes.

When we went out to warm up, we were greeted on the pitch by deafening jeers from the large, hostile crowd, jeers which only relented when we performed the show of respect for the audience that all Brazilian teams do: the whole team joins hand in a line, runs a few paces toward the main bulk of the crowd and raises their joined arms in a salute. It at least granted us a polite round of applause.

Our team was manifestly affected, either by nerves or the jeers, and started the game atrociously, much to the delight of the crowd. The riot police were taking interest in the crowd, along with some of their dogs. The police had to be especially attentive just 10 minutes into the game, when the crowd celebrated wildly a São Carlos goal scored from a mishit shot. Flares were lit as the colourful crowd – mirrored by a match ball of red, white and yellow – bounced around to the beat of drums. They were soon treated to another goal as Sorriso capitulated.

I couldn't believe that this was the same team who had so confidently dispatched all of our previous opponents in friendly matches. Gone was the spontaneous play, the joyful movement, the nutmegs. Andrei and Roger were unable to hold on to the ball up-front, meaning that São Carlos were able to put together wave after wave of attacks at Michel's highly penetrable goal.

Emerson reacted at half-time by altering the formation to an unorthodox 3-1-3-3, moving Furlan into central midfield. It removed all width and effectively killed any chance I had of getting on. Despite this I spent the whole second half warming-up, hoping that I would suddenly be given the nod. My every move was being tracked by a cameraman. Wherever I sprinted he followed, whenever I stretched he would focus in. My efforts came to nought, however. São Carlos scored twice more to make it 4-0. They really should have scored several more, but the referee took pity on us and turned down three blatant penalty shouts from São Carlos before blowing his whistle on exactly 90 minutes.

I guess Emerson's argument would be that he removed the width in the game to try and keep it tighter in central areas, with much of the traditional Brazilian style that São Carlos exhibited being about passing through midfield around the No.10, but I still didn't think he should have ignored the effect of offensive full backs that the game there so loved.

Back in the changing rooms the mood was subdued. We had managed one shot on target in the whole game, a speculative long range attempt from Leo. We had never been so dominated. Though few players survived from the previous youth team, Sorriso had won the Campeonato Matogrossense Under 18 title with an unbeaten record. We had come into the tournament with high hopes on the back of the support of the whole city. But we had been embarrassed. No, humiliated. We had let so many people down.

Luis called everyone into a circle. We performed our third rendition of the Lord's prayer since arriving at the ground, and Luis thanked God for ensuring that everybody finished the game fit and healthy. It didn't help. The team were still devastated. Chandler and Michel were both still in their boots and shin pads and staring at the floor by the time I had showered and changed. I don't know how long they stayed there but they only retreated to the stands in time to catch the second half of the Rio Branco – Palmeiras match.

A couple of the Sorriso suits were up with us, and I could tell that they were just as devastated as Chandler and Michel. It was they, after all, who had invested all that money into our team, an investment which had effectively been wasted in 90 minutes. Only one team in each group would progress from the group to the next round.

Palmeiras made light work of Rio Branco, beating them 4-1, a result which meant that to have any chance of qualification, we would have to beat Palmeiras, then thrash Rio Branco in our last game and hope that São Carlos dropped points. We had plenty of sunny, optimistic souls in our ranks but that might be stretching it even for them.

13

...AND DOWN TO EARTH

At least it wasn't a slow and painful death. Palmeiras confirmed our elimination both quickly and efficiently, dispatching us 5-0 in the torrential rain, which kept the crowd down to a few thousand when we had been looking forward to playing in front of a capacity crowd. We didn't even manage a single shot on target, our shortcomings exposed live on SporTV to hundreds of thousands of watching Brazilians. As soon as the first goal went in, we looked a beaten team, our heads going down as the flares went up. My abiding memory was of the Palmeiras goal scorers forming the shape of a heart with their hands into a TV camera, long before Gareth Bale adopted the celebration.

Again, my personal cameraman remained unsatisfied as I was confined to the substitute's bench for the entire game. The mood in the changing room was sombre. We had all been expecting this, but it hurt nevertheless.

It certainly hurt a man called Arif whom I was about to meet for the first time. He was a friend of Anderson's and lived in Peterborough, running one of the most successful Sunday League sides there, AK11, for whom Anderson had played. In return, Arif had agreed to Anderson's exhortations to invest in the Sorriso youth team. He had stumped up around £40,000 apparently and was mortified. After the game, he let out a sigh every now and again before returning his head to his hands.

We were a subdued bunch now, unlike the noisy group

full of life at Casa dos Filtros. We spent much of our time in our hotel rooms, watching a few English games on TV and highlights from the other games in the Copa São Paulo. I did venture out with Viniscius and Chandler to a shopping centre one day but I got bored with them trying on so many clothes, which were unlike European fashion and very expensive.

I also spent time in the hotel reception, waiting my turn to get on the internet on one of the two computers there, and talking with my new friend Kainun from the Rio Branco squad. As with Sorriso when I first joined, I was the main attraction for the Rio Branco players, and for their amusement I had to go through my routine of swearing in Portuguese and singing the sex song that Leo had taught me. The Sorriso players insisted that I add a new part to my routine, and I lost count of the amount of times the amused onlookers requested I said: 'Hello, I am Seth Burkett, not Boquet'.

Kainun was particularly mesmerised, and made a big effort to incorporate me into his team. As with the majority of Brazilians I met, Kainun was always happy, positive and full of laughter – he even embraced the nickname I gave him of *'Cagar'*, which has a similar pronunciation to his name and means 'shit'. He came from the Amazon, and had a passing resemblance to the Disney cartoon character of Mowgli from the Jungle Book. I was thrilled to see that he had more spots than me. They must have had underwear soap at their club too.

At least now, with the final match dead, I felt sure I would get a game, a feeling confirmed when Emerson put me on the 'good' team in training the day before, and told me that I would be starting. The trouble was that he made me play in central midfield, a position that was alien enough to me in English football, let alone in the smooth, silky, creative Brazilian game. Each of my mistakes was accompanied by Emerson screaming *'Ay caramba'* in disbelief, or *'porra'* (meaning 'ejaculate', a word that Brazilians use to indicate disgust). From this point it became obvious that I wasn't going to be starting.

I was amazed to discover on the lunchtime of the game, however, that I hadn't even made the cut for an already depleted squad, the two Leonardos both having left after the Palmeiras game – Di Caprio to a junior team in São Paulo and Leo to a professional side in the second division of the São Paulo state league. Instead, other fringe players such as Tallyson, a happy enough but quiet back-up striker who always kept himself to himself in Casa dos Filtros, Fernando, Leozinho and Lucas Castanhol were chosen ahead of me to get some game time.

Kainun had also found out he wouldn't be in the Rio Branco squad and together we headed into the reception area to vent our frustrations. I was in the middle of passionately telling Kainun how I hated Emerson's 3-5-2 system when I felt a soft hand on my shoulder. I turned round to see the man who often fronted the reception desk. '*Aqui*', he said, beckoning us toward the TV. He quickly looked left and right, to make sure that nobody else was watching. Happy that we were not being observed, he flicked the TV to a newly installed channel, number 79, with a beam on his face. *Playboy TV*. The man was thrilled. He had everything that made up Brazil in his hotel: football teams, Bibles in the rooms, samba music on the stereos and sex on the television.

Anderson looked genuinely surprised to see me in the stands at the game later that night, and gave me some kind, motivating words. Arif's business partner Marcio quickly managed to undo all of Anderson's good work: 'Emerson probably just wants to win the game', he assured me. I decided not to sit with Marcio after that, and positioned myself between the also omitted Luciano and Arif, directly behind Kainun.

Luciano had been the pleasant surprise of the tournament, exceeding expectations by keeping his requests to 'play game' at a minimum. Instead, he decided to add to his English vocabulary, and had argued with me for several hours that *boa noite*, meaning 'good night', actually meant 'good morning'. He argued so forcibly that in the end I had to accept that he was close enough and admit that yes, of course, *boa noite* meant good morning. Luciano took this as a personal conquest which confirmed his intelligence over me and I was pestered less by him. Everyone was a winner. Deciding that he had mastered the basics, he then attempted to learn how to count to 10 whilst watching the match. Arif, watching our team struggle again, was having a much worse time than Luciano, who was deep away in his own world and quite enjoying himself.

There was a bigger crowd for this game, mainly due to us being the warm-up for the sell-out São Carlos – Palmeiras game which would decide the group. The mood later would be electric for that but was more an atmosphere of quiet appreciation for us but with any skill, such as a nutmeg by Fernando, being greeted with roars.

Sorriso started the game well against a young Rio Branco side and were literally head-and-shoulders above them. We seemed certain to take the lead. Luis went down in the box and the referee pointed to the penalty spot. Finally Arif was about to get something out of his massive investment. Up stepped Andrei, top scorer in the Campeonato Matogrossense. Up rose the ball - all the way over the crossbar. Arif was stunned. He remained standing long after the ball was back in play, his mouth slightly open.

We looked good before the penalty but after it, reverted back to the team of our previous two performances. With every misplaced pass Arif let out a groan, every mishit shot resulted in a roar of anguish, and the inevitable Rio Branco goal was met with a mere whimper. The Rio Branco players were delighted that they were on course to win their first game.

They collapsed on the floor and raised their hands to the heavens thanking God.

A second goal soon followed, a goal which exposed Tallyson's shortcomings at left back. I afforded myself a wry smile. I wouldn't have let us concede that goal if I was at left back. Arif let out another scream of horror. His friend in England was streaming the game over the internet. He let him know that his team was awful at marking. 'Where are the strikers?! The left back is all over the place! Clueless, absolutely clueless!' he moaned, wondering where the skilled, creative team he had seen in training had gone.

I was especially upset to have missed the game because Emerson was finally playing with a back four, in the 4-2-3-1 formation that most of the teams at the tournament were using. I always felt I was more suited to the back four, which enabled me to break forward from deeper positions. I knew that I would have played well in this game and I struggled to watch it. I was so jealous of Tallyson, though in all honesty my plight wasn't his fault, and my anger was directed at Emerson.

If the dressing room had been sombre after the first two games then it was like a morgue after this 2-0 defeat to a very ordinary side. We still joined together to thank God for protecting us throughout the game, but this was the last major point of interaction between anyone until we arrived back at the hotel.

Only Fernando could hold his head up. He hadn't made the squad for the first two games, but Leo's exit gave him his chance and he had he seized it with both hands. Playing at right back, Fernando sauntered up and down the pitch, nutmegging opposing players at will. He was the one spark in a weary team, and his great skill brought roars of appreciation from the watching capacity crowd. Fernando's smile was perfectly justified, though I couldn't remember a time where I hadn't seen Fernando smiling.

In polar opposition was Arif, who looked like a ghost. Who could blame him, though? He had seen his 120,000 Reais investment concede 11 goals and score precisely none. How could a team ranked as the best in the whole state of Mato Grosso sink to such levels?

We didn't hang around long. Fabrice had decided we would return to Sorriso immediately after our final game in the group stage. We managed just to see Palmeiras come from two goals down to defeat São Carlos 4-2 and progress to the next phase of the tournament. Then we were whisked back to the Terraco Perea, where we had a quick dinner and said our goodbyes. Anderson assured me he would sort out my situation and we embraced. Arif was still too devastated to talk to anybody.

After nearly two months of preparation, our Copa São Paulo was over in one embarrassing week, even if I couldn't be held responsible for any of it, though that was no consolation.

The bus was silent as we made our midnight flit. There was no Leo to make everyone laugh, no Leonardo playing his ukulele. Nobody was samba-ing down the aisle. Nearly everybody was staring into the nothingness of the night. As the bus pulled away from the Terraco Perea it felt like we were driving from a terrible nightmare, like we were spreading our wings to soar away from the darkness.

Thirty minutes later we were plunged right back into the nightmare. The bus spluttered a couple of times and then rolled to a halt. What symbolism. Who knew how long it would take to get going again. Or even where we – I – went from here.

14
A PROFESSIONAL DILEMMA

Despite the debacle, the bus drivers survived the wrath of the Chairman once we had finally made it home. To the best of my knowledge they were able to escape Casa dos Filtros with their full wages tucked safely into their pockets. Even the Chairman had to admit it couldn't have been their fault. Emerson wasn't so lucky. He was due to take charge of the professional side after the Copa São Paulo but now things had changed.

How could Emerson embarrass the Chairman like that? How could his team perform so poorly? But, worst of all, how could he not play Sefi? The whole of Brazil wanted to see Sefi play, and Emerson deprived them of that joy. Did he not understand how he could have cast the club further into the national spotlight? There seemed only one option for the Chairman: sack Emerson. That, at least, was what the Chairman told me.

To be honest, I'm not sure to what extent Emerson's dismissal was due to his refusal to play me. I'd say it was more that he was the unfortunate individual the Chairman decided to blame. We didn't find out about Emerson's sacking straight away. After 32 hours, and just two stops, we arrived back at Casa dos Filtros. It was 8am, and, shattered from the drive, we all decided to head straight to bed.

At midday we were awoken with orders that we were to eat at Andrei's father's restaurant. Our numbers were much fewer now. Several players were dropped off in Cuiaba, and a number more went from São Carlos back to their homes in São Paulo or to the airport. Fabrice arrived to drive the bus, and in classic Fabrice fashion we made it in record time. The bus remained subdued, however. There were no cries of '*vamos motorista*' and nobody shouted at the unemployed men as we pulled into Sorriso. The Copa São Paulo had had an impact on Fabrice too. He looked older and less comical. He didn't greet me with his customary 'I farted'. He did not laugh at all.

It was at lunch that we learnt of Emerson's fate. The Chairman came over just as we began to tuck into our rice and beans to tell us of his decision. There was no emotion in his face or voice. Chandler laughed incredulously. If Emerson was sacked then that placed a question mark over all of our futures. Would any new manager want those fortunate enough to be selected by Emerson for the senior team? Would we be cast away like unwanted waste? It was quickly decided that we had to go and see Emerson right away. Viniscius knew where Emerson was staying (of course he did, how else had he managed to worm his way into the starting XI each game?) and we were all to follow him immediately.

I followed reluctantly. I had mixed feelings. I had been angry with Emerson for not playing me at the Copa São Paulo, though my nature is such that I was not going to confront him about it, but I was still sad for him. He had treated me well, by and large, and I enjoyed his training sessions. Now he was gone, would a new senior team manager want me? Then again, a new manager might play with a back four and I might have more of a chance.

The Chairman had taken me aside after breaking the news to the group to tell me of the influence I had had on his decision to sack Emerson. It took a while as, despite my new proficiency in Portuguese, the Chairman insisted on using his broken English to convey his reasoning. He knew a few of the

English words, 'Emerson no play Sefi' followed by a frown, 'All
Brazil want Sefi'.

He went on to assure me that I had a place in the professional side. Or at least I think that's what he meant. The Chairman had an annoying habit of throwing in the words 'problem',
'congratulations' and 'complication' at random points of
sentences, thus rendering them incoherent. And then there was
the added problem of Anderson. If Emerson had been sacked
then Anderson would not be so keen on me staying in Sorriso.
With Emerson there he knew I was safe. Without him there
was nobody to look out for me.

Anderson did not like or trust the Chairman. There was
something, shall we say, mysterious about how he had acquired
his money. His acquisition of such a stunning girlfriend nearly half his age was also a mystery, though I'd hazard a guess
his money was something to do with it. The Chairman's latest
actions were unlikely to alter Anderson's opinion of him.
Without Anderson's support following the sacking of his friend,
it would not be easy for me now.

After a 30-minute walk across the city we arrived at a hotel
consisting of a number of chalets set amid beautiful foliage
that was home to tropical birds. Clearly the coaching staff had
not been subjected to the same cramped, unhygienic conditions
that we experienced in Casa dos Filtros and I doubt their toilet
brush appeared on the kitchen table at meal times. I recognised
Emerson's shiny black 4x4 with tinted windows and person-
alised number plate parked up.

It had only been a few hours, but Emerson greeted us all
like old friends. 'Sefi!' he exclaimed when he saw me, shaking my hand then offering a warm hug. It was so warm that I
almost forgot the anger I had experienced two days previously
at not getting a game in the Copa São Paulo. After a long
discussion my team-mates all decided that they couldn't pos-

sibly betray Emerson by signing for the professional team at SEC. Emerson seemed pleased with the decision, and assured them that he would find them clubs.

He turned to me with his warm smile: 'Sefi, you come with me to São Paulo. We find you a club there.' I felt obliged to return his optimistic grin, but inside I was panicking. I wanted to stay in Sorriso. I did not want to sign for another junior team in a foreign city. I was used to Sorriso. I knew the city. I had friends here. I felt safe here. São Paulo was the unknown, a big city that would take much longer to adapt to, and it wasn't even certain that Emerson would be able to find me a team. Above all, the Chairman had said I was going to be given a pro contract here.

Despite that, I dutifully accompanied my team-mates when Emerson informed us that we had to pick up our documents from the Club President's house, which was back on the other side of Sorriso. This time the walk took 45 minutes in the blistering sun. I yearned to be back in Casa dos Filtros enjoying a siesta. This was no time for a pasty white Englishman to be trudging around in flip-flops on a wild goose chase.

The President wasn't in and even if he was, we were told, he couldn't help us as he didn't have our documents. Apparently the Chairman had them but I wasn't backing many of my team-mates to get much sense out of him. Whatever happened, it looked like I was staying in Brazil. I certainly wouldn't be able to fly out of the country if it was all going to go wrong. I cursed myself for allowing the Chairman to look after my passport.

We didn't get to see the Chairman until dinner, for which we returned to Andrei's father's restaurant. The Chairman said that Fabrice had the documents. He also told Chandler that Emerson would decide whether I went to São Paulo or stayed in Sorriso. On hearing that, I must have showed my desperation when begging the Chairman to allow me to stay in Sorriso, but

I didn't care. He needed to see how worried I was becoming. The Chairman replied with what he had uttered that lunchtime: Sefi in Sorriso was 'OK'.

The Chairman then banned me from going out and socialising with the rest of my team-mates, presumably because they had rebelled against him by visiting, and subsequently supporting, Emerson. My team-mates could not believe that I wanted to stay in Sorriso. They thought that I must have been over-exposed to the heat during our walk, that or I hadn't had enough sleep.

'But the President, the Chairman, criminals.' Chandler told me. Viniscius chipped in, 'They no pay your salary right, the players will rob you'. I didn't know why the players would rob me and suspected that Viniscius was exaggerating. My answer to both statements was simple: 'Please, professional, please'.

My team-mates didn't understand how I had always dreamed of being a professional footballer. For them it was easy. There are more than 800 professional teams in Brazil and they are all pretty open – if you are willing to pay or know somebody, then you can get a trial with any team you want, even the big ones. My team-mates could be professionals if they really wanted.

But I was from an English culture. There are only around 100 full-time professional teams in England, and they are all very exclusive. It is nearly impossible to get a trial at a professional club. They have to come to you, and getting noticed as a left back is a great deal harder than getting noticed as a 30-goal-a-season striker. Strikers have something statistical to be judged on, as well as subjective approval. As a left back, subjective approval was the only chance I had. Even if I was to be given a chance in English football I doubt I would be able to take it. The English game, based around physical attributes, did not suit me. My game, once I had properly adapted to the Brazilian environment, was much more suited to a Southern European or South American style (though not particularly suited to Emerson's unorthodox formations with three centre halves).

Neither did my team-mates realise how hard I had worked, and the big step I had taken in coming here, just to get myself into a position to make my dream come true. Being released previously had hurt. A lot. I've never cried as much as the day that I was first let go by Peterborough United. Even though I gave up on achieving my dream after being released by Northampton Town, I couldn't let go of football. Being told I wasn't good enough was painful. I had to do something.

And so every evening back then I took my ball into the garden (much to Mum's annoyance as her flower beds were trampled once again), and practised for a minimum of 45 minutes. I knew what was wrong. Northampton released me because I wasn't good enough on the ball. I was scared of having it at my feet and lacked composure. In essence I was a typical English player.

I would do kick-ups every day to improve. By the age of 16 I could do more than 5,000. The bulk of my practice time was spent doing basic dribbling activities, running up and down the garden using the soles of my feet or moving the ball diagonally between feet. Slowly but surely I became more confident on the pitch, and by the time I was offered the chance to play for Sorriso I felt that a comfort on the ball was one of the strongest aspects of my game.

Even when travelling to Brazil I knew that I probably would not have a long-term career in football. Even now, with the potential offer of a professional contract, I knew that I would not. I was sure I would go to university sometime soon. But I wanted to have the experience of being a professional foot-baller more than anything. To be honest, I didn't even care if I played in any games or not. All that mattered was that I signed a contract which meant I could class myself as a professional footballer. I had been getting paid to train and play full-time in the youth team, which could be classed as professional, but I felt that to truly fulfil my dream I had to become a pro for a senior side.

It was why I was willing to overlook the 'foibles' of the people running the club. It felt that I may never get this close again to fulfilling my childhood dream and had to take it. But could I take it? The Chairman was liable to change his mind at the drop of a hat, and if I fell into his bad books there would be no chance I would be allowed to stay in Sorriso.

My team-mates could tell that I was worried, and embarked on their old hobby of winding me up: 'Tomorrow, you go São Paulo. Anderson said.'...'Three days. You go England. Emerson said,'...'You come to my house in Florianopolis. We play there together. My dad said.' The most ridiculous statement came from Luis, who claimed that I was due to sign a contract in Qatar. When I contested it with him he nodded, wide-eyed, 'Emerson said!' I knew that they were winding me up, but the uncertainty was still eating away at me. I felt as though I had gone, in the space of 12 hours, from a guaranteed professional contract to the unknown, with no way of getting out of the country and an uncertainty of where I would sleep the next night.

As I had done when I landed in Brazil on my own, I suddenly felt my youth. I was just a kid... What was I doing here? I should have been with other 18-year-old English kids, playing computer games and worrying about essay deadlines. I was isolated and vulnerable. There was only one person in the world who could put me right. 'As long as you've got somewhere to sleep you're fine,' my Dad told me without the slightest hint of worry in his voice when I phoned him. He almost seemed a bit frustrated that I would dare to worry about such a trivial matter.

I awoke the next morning still fretful. The trio of players who were supposed to leave for Rio de Janeiro the previous night were still here, all in the dining area, eating their crusty bread rolls and drinking the usual warm chocolate milkshake. I had never seen the dining area so filthy. Usually it was only the bathroom in such a state. The dining room was cleaned fairly regularly, even if it did often play host to the toilet brush.

Indeed, the whole house had been descending into a fertile breeding ground for bacteria since we arrived back from the Copa São Paulo. The light in the bathroom had broken, prompting the Chairman to buy candles. But my team-mates, without any training to keep them occupied, were bored. Their new favourite hobby was to carry the lit candles around Casa dos Filtros and spray deodorant through them at regular intervals. I was amazed that nothing ever caught fire.

With the bathroom light out of action, the whole process of aiming at the toilet became more difficult and faeces appeared on the walls of one of the cubicles and the floor of another. Back in the dining area both the table tennis table and dartboard were broken. I suspect that the latter had something to do with Viniscius using the assortment of butchers' knives in the kitchen rather than the traditional darts.

The worst smell in the whole house came from the kitchen. No washing-up had been done since we returned from São Carlos, the situation made worse by the milk consumption in the house and the tendency to not drink the whole glass. The bulk of the horrible smell came from the storage. The kitchen wasn't cleared when we left for São Paulo, and remained uncleared. Rotten fruit littered the spare cupboards and fridge, giving off a disgusting stench.

I retreated to the cleanest area of Casa dos Filtros – my bedroom – and was thrilled to see on my phone that Anderson had tried to phone me. I rang him back, and was delighted when he picked up. He informed me that yes, I could stay in Sorriso if I really wanted but he would recommend staying with Emerson. I repeated my desire to stay in Sorriso, and Anderson assured me that it would be fine. The sky was becoming clearer, but the cloud would still linger until the Chairman would actually let me sign a contract.

Unwilling to return to the horrific smell, I lay on the bed and allowed Anderson's words to sink in. I even afforded myself a smile before getting on with my day. The previous night Dad advised me to hide my money. What with the number of players leaving, most of whom I'd never see again, the chances of my belongings going missing would naturally increase.

Under Dad's orders, I had hidden my money after each month but it now appeared that I hid it so well that I could not find it. From a rough calculation, I guessed I'd spent 350 Reais since arriving in Brazil, the bulk of which was on a necklace for my sister. I came to Brazil with 200 Reais, and had since earned 750 from SEC. That should have meant that I had 600 Reais, yet I could only find a quarter of that amount. Still, I didn't realise when I arrived that I was going to get paid, so I couldn't really be too upset.

With Emerson gone and the players in limbo, the only formal things to occupy us were the visits to Andrei's father's restaurant for meal times. Now we were joined by the professional team, which had been assembled for the forthcoming season and who were deep into their pre-season for the Campeanato Matogrossense.

They sat on the other side of the restaurant and I was in awe of them. They looked so... so Brazilian. All had athletic builds and gave off the aura of professional footballers. I felt intimidated by the laid-back ease with which they conducted themselves as they wandered round the restaurant in their flip flops and vest tops, laughing with the staff and their team-mates.

Then, one lunchtime, four days after returning to Sorriso, the Chairman called me over to his table.

'Ah, Sefi. Problem,' he said. My heart sank.

The Chairman must have seen the disappointment in my face, as he quickly retraced his steps. He emphasised that it was fine for me to be professional with SEC, but told me that there was a minor problem with my visa. I would have to go home to England for a week and then return to Brazil. My mum was always telling me that a week is a long time in football. In Brazilian football a week is then an eternity. If I went home, I may never get back out here, what with all the bureaucracy involved, and the Chairman's attitude towards it.

Six hours later, the situation changed again. I was helping myself to a dessert of acai, a purple berry fruit found in the rainforest and the best food I have ever tasted, when the Chairman approached me again. I would not have to go to England after all, he said, and I could move out of Casa dos Filtros tomorrow if I liked. Actually, I'd best move out of Casa dos Filtros now as my first session with the professional side would be tomorrow, and I'd need to leave for training with them from their hotel.

I needn't worry about the visa, he assured me, he had contacts in the federal police and they could sort it 'no problem'. My money was to double to 600 Reais a month. A contract would be drawn up for me to sign but I had signed a registration form for the youth team that covered me playing for the senior team so I needn't be concerned.

I should have been elated but I had been told so many different things that I remained sceptical. I also knew the Chairman could change his mind in seconds. I would wait until actually being part of a training session before allowing myself to be happy or excited. As well as feeling a little intimidated, I was also intrigued. How did the professional squad live? What were their attitudes, on and off the pitch? Would I fit in?

Fernando, Tallyson and Pelezinho left for Rio that evening. Viniscius soon followed them, though he was heading for his home in São Paulo. I would miss Fernando the most. His attitude towards life was truly inspiring, and his positivity was infectious. I wouldn't miss his masturbation reports, however. The loss of this quartet left just six of us in the house: Chandler, Roger, Leandro, Rian, Daniel Lucini and me. They had certainly changed their tune. None was going to São Paulo with Emerson anymore. They were now all going to sign professionally and were moving into the hotel.

A week a long time in football? In Brazilian football, a day is a long time.

15
CAPONE AND THE GANG

Part of me was sad to leave Casa dos Filtros but that could only be sentimentalism. I certainly shouldn't have been sad as our new residence was a great improvement on the filthy garage I had previously called home. No longer were we living on the edge of a favela. Now we were in a hotel like the one Emerson had stayed in – a real promotion. Chalets were set among tropical trees where lived colourful birds. At the centre of the complex was a swimming pool, barbecue area and snooker table. Somehow I didn't think that we would be playing snooker with Luciano's roll-on deodorant as the cue ball. This was far too classy an establishment.

My optimism was unfounded, not for the first time when it came to the Chairman. I wondered why he had insisted on bringing mattresses and one of the bunk bed frames from Casa dos Filtros to the hotel and the reason quickly became clear. The six youth team players awarded professional contracts were to be crammed into a two-person chalet. The Chairman ordered Chandler and Leandro to get to work on building the bunk bed, and unceremoniously dumped the remaining mattresses on the floor. They only just fitted. At least we had an en-suite toilet and a television.

The situation could not have been more different for the other professional players, with no more than two to a room. The players who were deemed to be the best in the team weren't even in the same hotel as us but in a much better one. At lunch

I was introduced to my new team-mates. As with every group of players I had been around, they all took a great interest in me, but I was more nervous around these. I used the same tactics as I had with the youth team to try and get them to accept me and went through my repertoire of swear words in Portuguese and singing. The requests for an encore were fewer with them, though – probably a sign of a bit more maturity through seniority.

Junior goaded me the most. He kept on nudging me and telling me to let his fellow striker Trevor know that he had a '*nariz grande*', a 'big nose'. I looked Junior up and down. He was the one with a massive nose. He also had long ears and braced teeth. Despite this, his smile was infectious, and it proved impossible not to be smiling in his company. I let him know that his own *nariz* was pretty *grande*, much to Trevor's delight. The pair of them were definitely the jokers of the team – Trevor's smile was just as infectious as Junior's, though it was hard to take seriously a grown man with a tattoo of Donald Duck on his arm.

I got talking to Leonardo, a man in his early 30s who spoke good English and had the whitest teeth I had ever seen. He looked like a surfer. Leonardo had spent much of his career playing in Europe, first leaving Brazil at the age of 17 to sign for Bundesliga club Hannover 96 FC. After eight years in Germany he went on to play in France and Switzerland. I asked him what position he played. Left back. Great. And it got worse. Alemao was also a left back. He played in the same São Paulo youth team as the great Kaka of Real Madrid, Milan and Brazil, and was playing for Coritiba in the Brazilian Serie A as recently as two seasons previously. It immediately looked like my game time was going to be limited.

Neither Leonardo nor Alemao was the most successful player in the team, however. That accolade fell to Capone de

Oliveira, the club captain. Capone was getting on a bit and didn't look to be in great health. His stomach was only just smaller than the Chairman's. His weathered skin suggested that he must have been at the wrong end of his 30s, though the packet of cigarettes he smoked every day might have had something to do with that.

But it didn't matter that Capone liked a drink, smoked and ate whatever he wanted, because Capone was a UEFA Super Cup winner and I have to admit that I was pretty star-struck myself. He had such an aura. I remembered watching in dismay as his Galatasaray side defeated Arsenal on penalties to win the UEFA Cup in 2000. For Capone the tournament had been bittersweet. He had scored in the previous round against Leeds United, but it went almost unnoticed in the pall cast by the stabbing to death of two Leeds fans the previous night.

The highlight of Capone's career was not the UEFA Cup win, however, but the subsequent victory in the UEFA Super Cup against Real Madrid. Playing at right back, Capone was able to keep his good friend Roberto Carlos quiet, and Galatasaray eventually triumphed 2-1 with a golden goal in extra time. Now that he was older and less fit, Capone was unable to make his lung-bursting runs up and down the right flank, so he dictated the play from the less physically demanding position of central defence.

Capone's unhealthy lifestyle was not the only baggage he came with. His signature marked a four-for-the-price-of-one deal. If Capone signed, then his two sons and cousin signed too. It wasn't too bad a deal, to be fair. His eldest son, Gustavo, had just returned from a Turkish Premier League side after leaving over salary disagreements, his cousin Andre, though unable to speak any English, spent time playing for Newcastle United as a youth, and his youngest son, Iago, had been on the books at São Paulo as a midfield player.

Iago spoke good English, which he told me he had learnt in the numerous international schools he attended as he followed his father's football career around the world. He was not attending school currently. He was going to train as much as he could, for both the senior team and the youth team as they began their preparations for the Campeonato Matogrossense. And it looked like Iago needed all the training he could get. Even though he claimed to earn 3,000 Reais a month as an under 15 at São Paulo (this must have been exaggerated), he had certainly taken his father's genes. He was chunky, almost fat. Even his face was a bit chubby, and his fat cheeks, combined with two large front teeth, gave him the appearance of a beaver. It looked like Iago was going to take Yago's place as my Google translate.

Capone must have earned a fortune from his football career, so I was surprised to see him lacing up a pair of Adidas F10's in my first training session. Now, F10's are the cheaper, 'fake' version of F50's. If anyone wore F10's in a professional environment in England they would be ridiculed. You could not be considered a good player if you wore 'fake' versions of the boot. All good players in England wear expensive, real boots.

The Brazilian government are not stupid, however. They know that they have nearly 200 million football fanatics living in the country, many of whom would love to purchase football boots. In England we tax alcohol and cigarettes. In Brazil they tax football boots. And so it is that a pair of F10's would set you back 230 Reais (around £75), a figure nearly three times their cost in England. It was only Penalty boots, a Brazilian brand, that were relatively affordable.

Because of this, good players in Brazil are allowed to wear pretty much any boots they like without it counting against them. Most of the professional players did just that, and over half were wearing the 'fake' versions of boots. There was only

one unwritten rule regarding football boots in Brazil: Bad players wore black boots, good players wore coloured boots. I
looked down at my black Copa Mundials next to the plethora
of white, blue and gold boots.

I felt that my black boots were very apt for training with
the professional side as I set out on the first session with trepi-
dation, and a bit of relief that I was actually here, even if a
contract had not materialised yet. They made the youth team
look like a load of pub players. Their skill, creativity and
physical attributes were all so much better. I was severely out
of my depth, and felt helpless in the middle of the *Rondos*
circle. As with the youth team, every session was started with
Rondos, and as with the youth team every player was immensely
comfortable with the ball at their feet, meaning that the
constant stream of nutmegs I received continued.

In my early days in the country, I had suffered from the
mistaken English idea of *Rondos* at first, and left my team-mates
exasperated as I admired another pass to the other side of the
circle. Once even Fernando shouted at me. Slowly I learned and
became more Brazilian by the day. Or so I thought. Capone
and his chums brought me crashing back down to Earth. To
Englishness.

A series of running drills followed the *Rondos*. It was pre-
season, after all, and the coach, Mosca (a nickname, meaning
'The Fly'), intended to work us all hard. Mosca had won the
Campeonto Matogrossense the previous year with Luverdense,
and he did not plan to relinquish the trophy quickly. We were
allowed Sunday afternoons off. That was all. The rest of the
week we were training: 13 sessions a week.

Mosca had to drill and organise his new players quickly. As
is customary in the lower reaches of the Brazilian professional
system, clubs sign whole new teams of players each season.
After playing in their state leagues early in the year, some clubs

do not enter the state cups in the second half of the year and so there is a lot of player movement. Of Mosca's 35-man playing squad, only two were registered for the senior Sorriso side the previous year, and these were both youth team players.

As for his own position, Mosca was unlikely to be back at Sorriso for the next season, and even if he was, then only one or two of his current players would be. Everything was this season or bust. Even the Chairman was only in it for the short-term, just a few years, then he would move on. The Club President and a few of the suits were the only mainstays at Sorriso Esporte Clube.

Whereas Emerson emphasised ball work, Mosca believed that players needed fitness. Of course musicians could practise without their instruments, what a daft statement. Why would a footballer need to do running with a ball? It was almost like I was back at Stamford. Fortunately, Mosca did allow us to see a ball after his excessive running drills, and split us into two teams in a possession drill.

We had been playing for less than two minutes when it happened. Leonardo gave me a short pass, which greatly inter-ested Capone, who was playing on the opposition. The only trouble was that Capone was still quicker in his head than in his legs, which just didn't move as he wanted anymore. I got there first, caressing the ball with my sole. I knew that I had a fraction of a second. He was coming at me quickly, his leg closing in on me, ready to dispossess the ball from the sole of my foot. I did it without thinking. My sole pushed the ball forward. It carried on going. Right between the gap Capone had left between his left and right leg as he went in for the tackle. In my head, I froze. I offloaded the ball as quickly as possible.

What had I just done? My mind went back to my first training session with the men's team at Stamford when I was just 16 and did the same thing. The club captain, a seasoned non-League man in his mid-30s, had been the victim of a nutmeg in a possession drill. The next time I received the ball he let me know his feelings, venting his anger at a kid who had made him look stupid by responding with two feet worth of studs to the shins. I couldn't walk properly for the next two weeks. I never nutmegged him again.

But here I was in luck. Capone was Brazilian. I hadn't made him look stupid, I merely exhibited a competent skill. He put my mind at ease as soon as the drill was over. 'Hey *Inglese*', he nodded approvingly and gave me a high-five and a thumbs up. What an honour. It went even further on the bus journey back home – I was invited to the back seat with the heavyweights: Trevor, Junior, Leonardo, Alemao and Adilson, the latter a figure with a sinister past, I would find out. Capone and his family didn't travel on the bus. The Chairman deemed them too important. Capone was allowed to drive back to his hotel in his 4x4, and nobody begrudged him that. Capone could do pretty much whatever he wanted and we would all still love him.

That first session proved to be one of the only times we saw a ball in my first week of training. After spending the first 15 minutes playing *Rondos*, the balls were all put back in the bags and we were sent off sprinting around various assault courses. One particularly warm afternoon we were forced to do 96 sprints. And these were not just simple sprints. They were split into eight different stations, ranging from sprints of 10 to 50 yards depending on the difficulty of the physical test which preceded it.

The jumping station was the hardest. Mosca had a string suspended half a metre above the ground, over which we had to jump continuously sideways before sprinting 30 yards. It was the closest I felt to death since the Vitoria days, though it was reassuring to know that I wasn't the only one struggling. 'All this training, it is very tiring', moaned the self-styled 'King of

Love', Trevor. 'It makes masturbating very hard. I am too tired to please myself'.

I guess, in hindsight, that Mosca would have been unsure about the differing fitness of his players and needed to get them all up to speed. Some had been playing in the national leagues finishing just a month ago in the December but others had not played since the state championships finished the previous April. And the season would be intense once it started. Fifteen teams had entered the Campeonato Matogrossense and we were in a group of eight, which meant 14 games in seven weeks and then a knock-out phase for the top four in each group after that.

Perhaps Mosca was thinking also that the older players were in more need of fitness training rather than ball work, their technique honed years earlier. Even so, I found it all at odds with previous Brazilian training sessions, having witnessed the Bahia senior side doing plenty with the ball during a session I saw when in Salvador the previous summer.

It was not just the physical workload that increased. We now prayed before every single training session, meal and bedtime. Led by Capone, we would all join hands in a circle and close our eyes whilst reciting the Lord's Prayer. I felt a real pressure to join in and decided to use my best experience of attending a Church of England primary school to recite the Lord's Prayer in English. At first they found it funny, and loved the fact that I was making an effort.

I soon got the impression, however, that the joke had run its course, and concentrated on listening to the slow, soft chant and memorising the words. I only ever managed to get as far as the first two lines: *Pai nossa, que estas nos seus, santificado sejo o teu nome...* then the rest of it was indistinguishable.

The prayers meant a great deal to a number of the players. Acassio, a centre back with long, straggly brown hair, stayed pointing toward Heaven with his eyes closed for a good 30 seconds after everyone had murmured 'Amen'. Diego, yet another left back, always looked like he was about to burst into tears. A handful of players would kiss the turf after. The vast majority would cross themselves and blow a kiss toward the heavens.

Dida would kiss his cross three times and then take a minute to himself. He was one of the most fanatical in the whole team. As a goalkeeper he was allowed to wear his own shirt to training – he had three T-shirts, one was emblazoned with 'Feliz 2000' to celebrate the millennium, one read '100% Jesus', and the other had a verse from John written across the chest. The 100% Jesus one was his favourite.

If training was anything to go by, we were going to be the fittest, most devout team in the league, that was for sure.

16
GAY VIEWS AND INTERVIEWS

I thought I was finished with Casa dos Filtros but the Chairman had other ideas. After the first week of eating our meals at Andrei's father's restaurant, he must have had a brainwave and realised that it would be cheaper to hire someone to cook for the team. And so it was that each mealtime we crammed into the Chairman's small Fiat Punto and travelled across the city to the home of the youth team.

It wasn't just food that the Chairman wanted to save money on, it was petrol too. Aiming to make as few journeys as possible, he stuffed his car with footballers until there was not even enough space to move. Our record was 11 people: one driver, two in the front passenger seat (one sat on the other), five on the back seat (Rodrigo was only 5ft tall, and could lie across the laps of four others), and three in the boot. Those in the boot were so squashed together that the Chairman had to drive around the city with his boot open, allowing the passengers to dangle their legs over the exhaust pipe.

You'd have thought that the police would have taken a special interest in the car but not so. They definitely clocked our overcrowded car – a large police station was located opposite our hotel, and we had to drive past to get to Casa dos Filtros – but there was no sanction from them. Indeed, there would always be a couple of policemen sitting outside the station and they would always give us a merry wave as we passed.

Casa dos Filtros was still the same. The junior Campeonato

Matogrossense was due to begin at the same time as the senior competition, and a whole new batch of youth team players were now billeted there. Charles, the midfield player who had not gone to the Copa São Paolo, and Leozinho were the only two youth-teamers who remained from our old team and they both lived in the city anyway so had no need to visit Casa dos Filtros.

Felipe was the only person living in Casa dos Filtros that I knew, but his stay was not going to be a long one. Despite being our third-choice goalkeeper for the Copa São Paulo, he had been awarded a professional contract with the senior side. The only trouble was that there was no space for him in the hotel, and so he had to bide his time until a member of the senior team decided to leave. Felipe was an adept keeper, but he was not a world-beater. Emerson had preferred both Michel and Bruno. But it was not Felipe's ability which had landed him the professional contract. Felipe was an orphan. Rather than move between foster homes and orphanages, Felipe moved between football clubs.

One other figure I recognised, who was now much more prominent in Casa dos Filtros, was Elias, the club director, who was in his late 20s. And it was not just in Casa dos Filtros that he was more prominent. He was everywhere – the senior hotel, training, matches. From what I could make out, he had taken up the role that Fabrice had done in the Copa São Paulo. The increase in work had not changed him. As soon as he first saw me he screamed 'Sefi' in his high-pitched voice, frantically waving at me before embracing me.

He greeted everyone else in just the same way. The senior players loved him. They called him '*boiola*', imitated his voice and slapped him on the rear. Trevor probably took it a step too far – he used to kiss Elias on the lips whenever he went past. The senior players liked being able to have a laugh with him about it and he loved the attention. Most important, though, Elias had a good heart. He would go out of his way to help anyone.

I suppose Elias's in-your-face homosexuality was accepted because he was a club official rather than a player. That might have been a different matter. Given my fellow youth-teamers comments about people being gay, my impression was that footballers in England and Brazil were equally homophobic.

Dressing room talk in both countries is frequently about women – degradingly so – and references to being gay – 'What are you, gay?' in England and '*viado*' in Brazil if you don't go in for tackles or show conventional manliness – are insults. To be gay would be to isolate yourself from the main social group which is one reason why those who have declared as gay have mostly done so after their playing careers have finished.

To come out, a player would have to be extremely confident in himself and his sexuality, particularly in Brazil. One player who certainly was confident was Liam Davis, who would, laudably, openly speak about his homosexuality at the age of 23 when a player at Gainsborough Trinity of Conference North. I played against him for Stamford when he was at Brigg Town and he seemed very comfortable with his sexuality.

Where the countries differ most is in the outward expression of contempt towards homosexuality in chanting by supporters, which is very open in Brazil. I noticed it in Sorriso but it was even more obvious higher up in the game where the names of the opposition players are better known. At their announcement, and that of the referee, up would go the cry of '*viado*.' Nobody complained. This is a country, after all, where Marco Feliciano, the elected president of the Commission for Human Rights and Minorities, would instigate legislation known widely as the 'Gay Cure'.

Aggression towards perceived homosexuality can be fierce.

In recent years, the Corinthians striker Emerson, a notoriously flamboyant, outspoken individual, posted a photograph on Instagram of himself kissing his friend on the lips – a male friend. All hell broke loose. Fans demanded that he be sacked, the more rabid even saying that he needed shooting. Banners appeared at games reading: 'Corinthians is a place for real men', 'Go and kiss a woman', and 'We don't accept homosexuals'.

There were similar reactions to the case of Richarlyson, a player for São Paulo. In 2007, a Palmeiras director insinuated on TV that Richarlyson was gay. Though this was not based in fact, a belief persisted that he was homosexual, forcing Richarlyson into a denial. Still, such was the feeling amongst some Brazilians that when Palmeiras attempted to sign Richarlyson they faced a backlash. Supporters confronted the Palmeiras directors, urging them not to sign a homosexual.

More ridicule was to follow for Richarlyson. He took Jose Cyrillo Junior – the Palmeiras director who made the assertion – to court for defamation of character, where he was told by the judge that Brazilian football was a virile, masculine sport and not a homosexual one. The judge said that Richarlyson could simply go on the same show and deny that he was gay. Failing that, he could keep quiet about being gay, but if he kept quiet and was gay he should quit the sport anyway.

One gem from the judges ruling was: 'What is not reasonable is the acceptance of homosexuals in Brazilian soccer. They would harm the uniformity of thinking of the team, the togetherness, the balance, and the ideal. By the way, this popular saying is very precise: Each one in their own area, each monkey in their own branch, each rooster in their own coop, each king in their own deck of cards. That is what I think, and because I think like this, in the condition of a judge, I say it!'

Richarlyson has since had to suffer relentless abuse throughout his career, though perhaps things might be changing in wider society even if more slowly in football. Not long ago, a popular Brazilian soap opera – and soaps are massive in Brazil, nearly as big as football – showed a gay kiss. The kiss was celebrated with cheers in bars in some of the more bohemian areas of the country.

Some time later I would discuss the subject with Yago and his take on it surprised me. In his experience, he said, one in five footballers was gay, but they keep quiet as they did not want to appear to others as if they had lost their masculinity. He claimed that about half of footballers were OK with gay players, half were not.

He added that there had always been at least one bisexual player in every team he had played on. He said it was because players lived together in dormitories like Casa dos Filtros from a very young age. They grew up together. They experienced puberty together. Naturally they would experiment, he said. Yago also believed that their poverty, their need for comfort wherever they could find it, played a part in their sexuality, their desires. Other players I spoke to disagreed with Yago's statistics and theories though they did accept that there would be vilification of any player who 'came out'.

Anyway, It wasn't long before I needed Elias's help. Back in São Carlos at the Copa São Paulo, I had done an interview with a Brazilian journalist. The journalist was quite young and I hadn't thought much of it. It was only when the subsequent article appeared on every news site in Brazil that I became intrigued, a feeling that was soon replaced with worry. The journalist obviously had an agenda, and I cursed myself for having such trust in him and being so honest.

'Seth Burkett did not expect to worry about his clothes on the 25th December', the article read, 'but upon arrival in Brazil, the young Englishman encountered problems due to the carelessness of the Sorriso staff... He received his clothes back from washing full of holes, and wanted to buy new ones, but he couldn't. "I'm not allowed to go out to the city centre because of the bang bang," he said.'

The article got worse. The journalist had used the photographs I had posted on my Facebook page. The lead photograph with the article was a picture of the filthy bath-room facilities and was captioned to let the audience know how disgusted I was. My Facebook page was not the only link that the journalist found. My Twitter page also provided material, and the journalist was especially interested in the tweet that I foolishly sent after learning I wasn't in the squad for the Rio Branco game: 'Been dropped. Pissed off.' which he translated into Portuguese.

I wasn't sure whether it was the language barrier or the fact that he wanted to stitch me up. One or two of my T-shirts had come back from Oswaldo's wash with a couple of tiny holes in, but this certainly hadn't happened on Christmas Day. I had been warned that Brazil was a violent country and, as a foreigner, I would be at danger of being mugged. But I certainly hadn't said that I was not allowed outside. Maybe I'd told him the story of Third Street. I couldn't remember.

Either way, the Chairman was furious. Much worse than the time I'd ventured down Third Street, and who could blame him? How dare I talk about the club in such a manner? Why would I say these lies? I had made the club a laughing stock in front of the whole nation. Why have I complained about the bathroom? I was receiving the same treatment as Capone, a UEFA Super Cup winner, and I was a friend, a brother, a part of the Chairman's family, so this behaviour was unacceptable. Why would I do this when the Chairman had had to persuade the Club President to allow me to sign as a professional (not that I had; there was still no sign of a contract)? Why?

Elias, having seen the commotion, stepped in. It was just as well as I was sure the Chairman was about to crank up his rant. Elias took a while to calm the Chairman down. I imagined how it must feel to be a poor bus driver. Eventually, the Chairman put his hand on my shoulder. 'Errr, Sefi. I. Problem. You, write, errrr, problem. Story, complications. No true.'

I nodded. 'Sorry', I muttered, and I truly felt sorry. I had let him down. The Chairman must have realised my regret as his tone lost its harsh edge. Under Elias's guidance, we decided that I would write to the journalist telling him that his story was untrue and that I was issuing a formal complaint. The journalist never replied, but it did at least save me from the same fate as the host of bus drivers. For now.

There was at least one person who was amused by the 'bang bang' image of Brazil that I created in the article. Xuxa originated from a favela in Rio de Janeiro. Even though he had enjoyed a successful football career as a midfield player, including time at Santos, he still had family back in the favela that he visited fairly regularly.

'I gangster. Son of a bitch!' he cried in English, as he mimicked two guns firing into the air with a joyful expression on his face, his tattooed body shining in the sunlight.

'I kill you!' Trevor only wound him up further, pretending to shoot at him. 'Xuxa loco!' he approvingly roared.

One person who might actually have been loco was Adilson, though it was less immediately apparent with him. When I first met him, I thought the midfield player to be shy, quiet and unassuming. When spoken to, he would take his time to consider what had been said, deliberating on how best to answer, before delivering a calm, well thought-out point. There wasn't much of Adilson. He wasn't short, but he had a skinny physique. His skin looked weathered. Junior called him egghead, due to the absence of any hair on his head. Adilson didn't mind this and so, under great pressure from Junior, I also began to call him this.

As with all of the players, Adilson had read my 'bang bang' article. Trevor knew this, and one lunchtime he pointed in Adilson's direction. 'Err, Sefi. Adilson. Bang bang. Five years.' He held up five fingers with that wide cheesy grin of his. I turned to Iago for clarification of what I just heard.

'It's true, man', he told me, 'he came out of prison last year. Spent five years in there. Locked up in a São Paulo prison.' I turned to Adilson, who had a sheepish look, and asked him what he did. He lowered his head for a good few seconds. Eventually, he raised it:

'I shoot two guys... football argument.' Once again, I turned to Iago for clarification. Iago nodded.

No wonder Junior had been so insistent that I called Adilson 'egghead'. He must have found it hilarious. I didn't want to ask Adilson if the men were still alive. Was football really a matter of life and death in Brazil? I resolved to stay away from Adilson on the football pitch, though I hadn't yet had the chance to see him in training. I didn't know if he was injured, but he would always remain at the hotel when we went off to train.

Adilson assured me that he had changed. He had seen the light in prison and found God. He was safe. He wore the cross around his neck with pride day and night. He was a man of God now, he insisted. He never told me if he regretted his actions but one thing was for sure. I would not be calling Adilson 'egghead' any more.

17
NAME CALLING (2)

There used to be a centre half in one of the English teams I played for who refused to eat any of the black jelly babies. 'Why would I want any of the fucking darkies? Darkies have no fucking use,' he would growl, throwing the 'offending' sweets across the changing room floor. Our team had no black players. Playing in the Northern Premier League we rarely came across black players. To many of us they were just distant other people.

The centre half lasted two seasons. He was our best player, and the club put him on a lucrative (by non-League standards) contract. In the end, he got an offer from a better team and off he went. The black jelly babies never suffered such abuse again. He was the only one who refused to eat them. Everyone else accepted that they had just as much right to be in the packet as any of the other jelly babies, and would usually request that the centre half give them the black jelly babies. Actually, they were among the tastiest, certainly better than the orange and green ones.

People never see Brazil as being racist. Just one look at the make-up of any team would make such a suggestion laughable. The country is colourful and diverse. Whites, blacks, Indians, rich, poor, immigrants - they all come together to form an image of racial harmony. Sorriso had a great mix of backgrounds. So did all of the teams I came across.

In Brazil it is harder to see difference. There is no definitive white and black. Instead there are a range of colours, all blurred together, coming from years of inter-racial marriage and interaction between the numerous backgrounds of the Brazilian population. Thus is it difficult to define someone by their skin colour. Take Viniscius. If he was in Kenya, he would be considered white. If he was in Iceland, he would be considered black. Some days in Brazil he was black, some days he was white, depending on the perception and background of the beholder.

That doesn't mean that nobody in Brazil is considered black, just that there is more scope for what is considered black. A couple of weeks into senior training, midfield player Aroldo approached me. 'Hey', he said, 'don't call me Aroldo. We are friends. Call me *negao*.' It is a derogatory word for a black person, akin to the word nigger. He must have noted my surprise because he continued, 'I like being called *negao*. My friends call me *negao*.' For Aroldo, and for Brazilian culture as a whole, '*negao*' seemed to be used as a term of endearment. When I told him of the racial implications the word had in England he tutted. 'Here is OK', he assured me, putting his thumb up and smiling. I told him that sorry, I just couldn't use the word. In my culture it was unacceptable.

I would think of this episode some time later when the controversy arose over Liverpool's Uruguyan Luis Suarez calling the Manchester United left back Patrice Evra a similar word, but in Spanish. It showed up the cultural differences between South American and European attitudes, though clearly Suarez's term was unacceptable. He should clearly have been more sensitive to the culture he had come to, as I tried to be in Brazil. That, though, would not extend to mimicking the ingrained and casual racism.

Until the conversation with Aroldo, I had considered Brazil to be exempt from racism, my views formed from my time in Sorriso and Salvador. I saw Brazil as a model of racial harmony, with all cultures and ethnic minorities integrated into mainstream society. But Aroldo's request got me thinking. I remembered how Emerson had occasionally called the black members of our youth team '*negao*'.

Rian, for example, had the dark skin of an indigenous tribe member, meaning that he could be considered both black and non-black. More often than not, however, he was black. He would occasionally be referred to as '*negao*', and called the other black players '*negao*'. Whenever Rian said the word it was playful. When Emerson said the word it was more to grab the individual's attention.

In the senior team everyone called Aroldo '*negao*'. It was much easier than having to stumble over his polysyllabic name. But nobody called Ernandez '*negao*'. Ernandez, a goalkeeper, was just as black as Aroldo, but much bigger. He did not tower over the others – standing at six feet he was tall, but not a giant – but his physique dwarfed everyone else on the team. He weighed 17 stones. Nobody got on his wrong side.

Xuxa was the only white person I knew who came from a favela. When we drove past slums there were never any white faces. When we drove past gated communities there were rarely black faces. None of the SEC suits was black. All of the richest people in the youth team were white. All of the local governors were white. All of the street cleaners were black. Maybe there was a difference. The very fact that black people were called '*negao*' surely denoted that Brazilians were not colour blind. They saw difference.

I headed to the internet cafe that evening. I emailed my old Google translate for some help with understanding the issue here. 'Man, we have some racism but you hardly see,' Yago typed back. 'Since Brazil become a country we have blacks, and the slavery ended early so people today don't care. *Negao* isn't racist like it is in England or the US, for us it is the same as black guy. If you call *Preto*, that means black, sounds more racist, but it depend on the context and who you talk to. Some blacks don't care.' I was sure that the emphasis was on 'some'. As for slavery, well, Brazil was one of the last major countries to abolish slavery, waiting until 1888. Before then, Brazil had imported around five million slaves. The United States imported 400,000.

Football came to Brazil just six years after slavery was abolished, the sport introduced by Charles Miller, who was born in São Paulo of a Scottish father, a railway engineer, and Brazilian mother of English descent. Miller was sent to English public school at the age of 10 and returned to his birthplace in 1894 imbued with a love of football.

The country had not forgotten slavery, and retained elements of its influence. Championed by the white elite, football in Brazil adopted their values, acquiring a racist and exclusive character. The liberated slaves became intrigued by the sport, however. Banned from entering the grounds, they watched from any vantage point they could find. By 1910 football was the most popular sport in Brazil – on the one hand being a sport for the elite, on the other proving fun for the masses.

Many slaves moved to Rio following their liberation and began to play football, though not welcomed as the elite sought to keep the game as white and upper-class as possible. And it worked. Any black players fortunate enough to play in the state league were made to feel ashamed of their skin colour.

There was a story of an infamous incident with a player called Carlos Alberto, a man of mixed white and black heritage. Carlos would cover his face with powder before games to hide his skin colour, leading to one of the club's nicknames, *po de arroz* (meaning 'rice powder'), which opposition fans would chant when his make-up began to run off as he began to sweat.

There were some mixed teams. Bangu, near Rio, were founded in 1904 from Fabricia Bangu after some Englishmen who worked there had brought a ball to the factory. When they saw the enthusiasm the workers had for the sport, they decided to establish a club which was soon accepted into the Rio state league. Although the aristocratic clubs did not approve of the non-white players in the Bangu side, they did not see them as a threat to their hegemony. They allowed them to play in the league as long as their black opponents did not touch them on the pitch. It was unrealistic and when it happened, as it often did, the referee was under strict instructions to give a free kick to the white player.

The next big step in racial integration in football was made by Vasco da Gama, a club representing the Portuguese community in Rio. Vasco began in the smaller leagues, and eventually gained promotion to the Rio state leagues in 1922. What made them special was that they chose players regardless of race or social class. Most of their players were recruited from the smaller leagues from which Vasco had been promoted, and the mix obviously worked.

In 1923 they won the Rio state league with seven working-class whites, three blacks and a mulatto, the traditional term for a person of mixed parentage. The aristocratic Rio clubs were furious. They did not like how Vasco got around rules on amateurism - rules which also helped to keep out blacks and the working-class - by employing their players in their own shops.

The following season, the outraged aristocratic clubs in Rio pressured Vasco to ban players they did not consider suitable for the league. Vasco refused and the aristocratic clubs consequently created their own league, from which Vasco were banned. They held their ground and remained in the 'string league', which they won that season. The new league created by the breakaway clubs received the backing of the Brazilian Sports Confederation, and became the official league of Rio.

Vasco had great support, which applied relentless pressure to the aristocratic clubs. In 1925, the new league abandoned most of its racist conditions and Vasco were allowed to join. There remained one condition, however, which was designed to deter black and working-class players – all players had to know how to sign their names. Vasco, whose players were largely illiterate, got around this problem by sending their players to reading and writing classes. Flamengo may have won the championship in 1925, but Vasco had proved a point.

In 1933, Vasco helped to establish the first professional league in Rio. It not only signalled the end of amateurism, but broke the barriers of class and race, one team even fielding 11 black players in their opening game. Fluminense remained resistant. They would not accept black players in their squad for another 20 years. Slowly but surely, though, Vasco's vision became reality.

In the 21st century blacks and mixed race players are seen as an integral part of Brazilian football. It is those who learnt the game on the streets who are credited with the development of the *joga bonita* – the beautiful philosophy – of Brazilian football. It was this philosophy that was so evident at Sorriso, an environment of nutmegs, shimmys and turns. Blacks, mixed race and whites all played together in harmony. Even the coaching staff at SEC comprised two white men, two of mixed race and one black man. Of the seven players awarded professional contracts, Daniel Lucini and I were the only whites. Roger, Felipe and Chandler were mixed race. Rian and Leandro were black.

But racism still lingered, though was never admitted. There was a clear example of the Number 12 in the Brazilian women's national team. Her name was Pretinha. Her name translates as 'little blacky.' 'Some blacks don't care,' Yago had told me. Surely this meant that some blacks did care, and when Pretinha was on view to the whole world I wondered how they felt. Yago was white, of Italian descent, and, even if unwittingly, was part of the problem. Whites, it seemed to me, refused to admit that there was a problem with racism. Only once they recognised it, I felt, could they begin to work on eradicating it.

Brazilian football is no longer the plaything of the upper-class but cuts across all strata of society. And while I loved the way of playing, along with the racial integration, the more I read about and pondered the nature of life and the game there, and the more I experienced both, the more I began to grasp the nuances of the nation's attitudes and culture.

The latest census had revealed that 51 per cent of Brazilians considered themselves to be black or mixed race. On average, whites received slightly more than double the income of black or mixed race individuals. Well over half of the people in Rio's favelas were black. Just seven per cent of the residents of the richer areas of the city were black.

Although blacks were prevented from becoming members of the aristocratic football clubs, Brazil never employed segregation nor had an organisation such as the Ku Klux Klan. A quick Google search revealed a quote from Brazilian sociologist Antonio Riserio: 'It is clear that racism exists in the US. It is clear that racism exists in Brazil,' he said. 'In Brazil, racism is veiled and shamefaced [Yago's refusal to admit it?]. In the US it is open or institutional.'

By all accounts, things were improving. The government had introduced racial admission quotas at universities to encourage them to take black people wishing to further their education. Measures were being implemented to improve equality in jobs. The biggest struggle, though, was changing attitudes. Some time later I would read an article on *The*

Economist website which quoted a young Brazilian black man: 'If a black man and a white man go for a job, the white man always gets it,' he wrote. 'People look at a black person and immediately assume that they are of a lower social class than a white person. They are deemed lesser.' Despite this, Brazil still touted itself as the most racially diverse society in the world, a true racial democracy.

Football, at least, had come a long way in a century, the discrimination which plagued the game in Brazil in the early 20th century seeming to have disappeared. A player was certainly, in my experience, picked on his ability rather than his skin colour. Nobody had to powder their face in order to play.

Perhaps football, indeed, could set an example for Brazilian society as a whole. Maybe many in Brazil held the racist, misguided view that once seemed prevalent in Britain and the United States, that blacks were athletically superior but intellectually inferior, meaning that they can succeed on the football field but are disadvantaged in employment. But maybe attitudes were changing.

This latest census showed for the first time that blacks outnumbered whites, though the reality quite simply was that it had been so for many years. Behind this study was the probability that there was now less stigma attached to being black and that fewer of mixed race classified themselves as white, leading to filling in the form more honestly. Whatever the case, Brazilian society could learn from football's open door policy, and football could do with becoming less colour conscious.

In the meantime, in a country where players could be called by given name, family name or nickname, I would not be calling Aroldo Corazza by HIS nickname.

18
DAY OF THE DANCING DEBUT

January 23rd is a date that I will never forget. It is the date when my childhood dream came true, the date when I made my debut as a full professional, even if it was only a pre-season game away against Novo Mutum for some small cup. I had never heard of Novo Mutum but was told they were one of the top local amateur teams, from a town of 30,000 people. Two hours and 140 kilometres away was still considered local.

The day got off to a good start, with a number of major publications in Brazil carrying a story about me. The day before, my Dad had found a strange man snooping around the primary school where he taught and he confronted him. The man said he was looking for information on Seth Burkett and could he possibly have a word with St. John Burkett? He turned out to be from a news agency. Dad was thrilled that his boy was finally getting exposure after all of those petrol miles he had done to get him to training four times a week in Northampton.

He would be less thrilled when he got my phone bill some time after. After the Copa São Paulo, I had been down and he told me not to worry about the cost of calls home. That was until it reached £900, which qualified me for O2 gold membership. It should be said the majority of the cost was largely down to media requests. Today the phone was hot again, this time for happier reasons.

It was the Chairman who told me I would be in the squad travelling for the game. By now I had stopped asking him about a contract. I was just happy for now being involved in the senior team and I had food and accommodation. A piece of paper confirming my status would have been nice, but I was being paid.

I was pleased that I was to be in the squad though did not permit myself to be elated. There was some excitement in me but it all felt a bit unreal. I was in a bit of daze. And hadn't I been told at the Copa São Paulo that I would play and didn't? Perhaps that explained why I wasn't nervous as I usually am before a game. I would believe it when I experienced it. I might just be an unused substitute again. Still, I had been selected when a couple of the other youth-teamers hadn't so that was a bit of a feather in my cap.

Typcially, we left 90 minutes late for the game, Roger, Rian and Chandler from the youth team also in the squad. We arrived five minutes before the scheduled kick-off. Fortunately Novo Mutum were working on Brazil time too – they hadn't even arrived by then. Their changing rooms were being reno-vated and we were forced to change on the covered court for futsal located next to the pitch. They didn't have any dug-outs either, which wasn't ideal in the rain that was beginning to fall. Instead they had erected a gazebo, which all of the media and suits sat under alongside the fourth official. There was no room for any players. I knew I would be a substitute and would feel like I was back in Sunday league, standing on the sidelines with my arms crossed waiting to be subbed on.

Novo Mutum turned up in dribs and drabs, and were all there 10 minutes after we were scheduled to kick-off. They ran a couple of lengths of the pitch, kicked a few balls about and then declared themselves ready. Two of their players were wearing Astroturf trainers.

Metaphorically, Novo Mutum never turned up. The class between the amateur and professional side was enormous. It was like being back with the youth team in their pre-Copa São Paulo friendlies. The sheer skill and movement of the players was irresistible. You could hardly tell that we had been starved of footballs in Mosca's pre-season drills. Perhaps it was his strategy: to make us hungry for the ball. Our team looked like they had all covered their boots in superglue, such was the control. Alemao was nutmegging all and sundry and Leonardo was losing players at will. Capone eased in and out of the game when he desired, spraying the occasional diagonal pass before having a well-earned rest. It wasn't like he needed to do any defending.

Even in the wet conditions a crowd of around 600 had gathered. There were no stands, only a grass bank behind some advertising boards and a wired fence. One of the crowd members had brought a boombox the size of the Chairman's Fiat Punto, and it was his job to provide the atmosphere by playing samba music throughout the match. A small section of the crowd spent the whole game dancing.

On the pitch another 11 people also spent the whole game dancing: those in the green and white of Sorriso. A mesmerising dance it was too, overwhelming the Novo Mutum players with individual skill and fluid movement, twisting, turning dribbles. By half time we had a 3-0 lead. The third goal was very Brazilian. Leo Rosa – one of two locally based players on the team – dribbled past half of the Novo Mutum team from his position at right back before squaring for Alemao, playing at left back, to tap-in. Our old Stamford manager would have had a fit if he saw two defenders so far up the pitch, unless it was for a corner kick.

When Sorriso scored a fifth in the second half, Mosca turned to me. '*Inglese… Vamos,*' he croaked. He still hadn't learnt my name. I suddenly felt a great rush of adrenalin and the elation that I had denied myself earlier. I was ready to run through a brick wall for him and the team and complied eagerly with his request, declaring myself warm after a quick couple of sprints. I was going to make my professional debut and it could not have been in better circumstances. No matter how I played, I was pretty sure that Novo Mutum would be unable to score six goals in the 10 minutes left. And I was finally going to play in a back four. No more of Emerson's ineffective three centre halves.

The ball went out of play and the fourth official asked my name, checked who was coming off and allowed me then to validate my childhood dream. I sprinted on to the pitch before he or Mosca could change their minds. I had done it. I was making an appearance as a senior professional in Brazilian football – the only Englishman in the entire country of 3.25 million square miles and more than 200 million people to be playing professionally.

Roger and Rian were already on the pitch, and Acassio gave me some encouragement from his position at centre half. '*Joga bonita, Inglese*,' he urged. I appreciated it. Instead of my brick wall English mentality, I suddenly calmed down and sought to follow his instructions and play with the aesthetic qualities the phrase implies. My first touch in professional football was a simple ball down the line to Roger. I repeated it for my second touch. Completing two successful passes caused my confidence to soar and my nerves to disappear. My third touch in professional football would be altogether more complex.

The music was enticing my body into dance. Suddenly I was Brazilian, cutting inside to beat one man before performing a stepover past another. Out of the corner of my eye I saw Junior make a sharp movement. I reacted quickly, playing the ball between the two centre halves. Junior controlled it and lobbed the goalkeeper. Goal! An assist – I must have been dreaming.

But Junior's movement had been too sharp. The linesman

stood with his arm raised, his flag aloft. Junior was offside. There were no real complaints. We were 5-0 up and nobody was too fussed about missing out on another goal. My heart sank though, but at least I had created a 'goal' right in front of Mosca's eyes. Surely he must learn my name now. His blank face suggested not.

Those 10 minutes were the best I had played since arriving in Brazil. I played with the same joyful freedom of expression that the Brazilians do. *Joga bonita*. Every time I received the ball I felt my spirits lifted. The only thing that was missing was a nutmeg. It wasn't just my performance that impressed. In a break in play, the Novo Mutum right back, upon discovering my nationality, gave me a big hug. 'Much good', he smiled at me. Imagine seeing that in the Premier League.

The Chairman was waiting for me when I came off the pitch. I was ecstatic that I had played well in front of him after he had shown such faith in me. Maybe he would forget that damaging article now and just remember today's. He had a huge beam across his face.

'You debut professional. Very good!' he said and delivered the good news. He had spoken to Anderson for 20 minutes on the bus to the game, and together they had sorted me out. I would have a new visa next Monday. I now had a year-long professional contract. He asked if that was OK It was more than OK. I was delighted. I was living the dream.

There was even time for the day to get better. The Brazilians were samba-ing down the aisles in force on the drive home. They even got me up to try. Elias attempted to show me how, but gave up when he realised I had no rhythm whatsoever. We stopped on the way back for pizza, which had also been a post-game ritual with the youth team. We were met with more when we arrived back in Sorriso. It was my first ever taste of chocolate pizza, which proved to be one of the finest foods I had ever enjoyed. It seemed apt to finish my day with such a child-like food. It truly had been the stuff of childhood dreams.

Back in my room I was able to reflect in peace. My thoughts were racing, my smile enormous. We'd done it, Dad. All those years spent driving around the country, standing on cold, rainy park pitches. Those hours you'd made me go outside and prac-tise and practise and practise. Your sacrifice. My sacrifice. It was all worth it. We'd done it.

He was ecstatic when I rang him, even though it was late in Brazil and, three hours on, the early hours of the morning in England. I couldn't have done it without him. I had to tell more people. I had to track down the man who released me from Pe-terborough. I found an e-mail address on the internet. He was working for a new club now, one in the Conference.

'Not sure if you remember me', went the e-mail, 'but I played for your team as a nine and 10-year-old. Just letting you know that I'm now playing professional football in Brazil'. I didn't care if it was a bit premature. It felt great to have proved some-one wrong, especially when that someone had made you cry and cry and cry by saying you weren't good enough. I wished I was never released from Peterborough. To be fair, he replied some time later saying that he was pleased for me.

Then Bilf rang me. It was his birthday and Josh and Marco were celebrating it with him at his university. He was too drunk to listen to my news. All he could say was that he'd lost Marco and that Josh was going to have sex with his flatmate but he was angry with Josh because Josh had told him a fence wasn't electric and it was and it hurt and that he wouldn't care about any of this but he didn't have a clue where his glasses were. In fact, he couldn't remember having them all evening. I ended up speaking to him for an hour. His glasses turned up two days later. He was walking back from a lecture when he saw them balanced on a bush. Josh didn't have sex with his flatmate.

Mosca didn't let us get carried away. He scheduled a double session for the day after our emphatic victory, which was particularly painful for Roger and Chandler who had arrived back in our room at 5.30am. Being in chalets meant it was easier to break the curfew. You just had to walk through the front gates without being noticed. The morning session was an easy one. It was at the gym, and we pedalled on the bikes as we watched São Paulo beat Santos on penalties in the final of the Copa São Paulo from which our youth team had been so easily eliminated.

The afternoon session was much harder. We had to sprint a distance of 250 metres before getting a minute's rest, all repeated 20 times. If we took longer than 40 seconds to run the distance in any of the repetitions then it would not count and we would have to do it again. For Mosca, who still hadn't learnt my name, this was a session of moderate intensity.

Probably the hardest part of the session came at the very end. The kit man Tharik, from Mogi Mirim, like Capone, had been despatched by the Chairman in his Punto during the warm-up for the session. Now he had returned with a car full of ice blocks. His second-in-command, Batista, retrieved a large paddling pool from the changing rooms, and poured enough cold water into it to cover our legs. Tharik then dumped in the blocks of ice. Some were the size of an arm.

After training finished, Mosca forced us to sit in this ice bath for seven whole minutes. Considering that it was nearly 50 degrees outside, this proved to be hell. The pool could take six people at a time, and I felt for the first six who clambered in. All of the youth teamers got to go last, when a lot of the ice had melted. Eager to experience it for himself, Tharik climbed in with us. It was horrible. The cold rushed to my body like a throbbing pain. I had to divert my attention somehow. I bit down on my arm as hard as I could. It felt good. The feeling of cold lessened. I carried on biting, biting and biting.

Trevor was having fun. After finishing his ice bath he had looked down his shorts and exclaimed 'Oh my God, I am woman'. Now it was his job to inflict as much pain on us as possible, and he guffawed as he pushed all of the ice blocks toward me. That was the longest seven minutes of my life. The sheer relief when Mosca called time was overwhelming.

I wasn't the only one who was struggling. Tharik's legs had stopped working and he had to be hauled out of the bath. When he was put on his feet his legs collapsed from under him. They were bright pink. He lay there, like a tortoise fallen on to its back, whimpering for several minutes. It was the last time he'd get into an ice bath. We weren't so lucky. This turned out to be our new daily routine.

The team looked shattered on the bus. Some people were even asleep. The session, on top of the morning work and game the previous day, had really taken it out of us. We needed a rest. Trevor did his best to lighten the mood. He kissed a sleeping Chandler on the lips to wake him up before showing his bare rear to prove his point in an argument about cleanliness. Spotting that his partner in crime Junior wasn't looking, he moved his rear onto Junior's face, rubbing it against his *grande nariz*. Trevor lost the argument. His rear wasn't clean after all. I for one would be avoiding getting into arguments with Trevor.

19
BEYOND THE FRINGE

I couldn't put it off much longer. It had been over three months since my last haircut. Tharik insisted that he could cut hair, but I had resisted his offer for weeks. It was only when I saw him cutting Aroldo's hair that I finally gave in. My first task was to prevent him from giving me a Mohican. The Brazilians were still heavily influenced by Beckham's hairstyle at the World Cup draw, and many of them had copied him. Tharik had been advising me for weeks to follow suit and that he was just the man to do it. A Mohican was off the agenda, however.

He did it quite professionally, I have to admit. I entered his three-person chalet (which he had all to himself) and sat in the chair. He wrapped a sheet around me and off we went. After 20 minutes of careful attention, Tharik declared that he was finished. I was impressed but wondered when he was going to cut my fringe. He clicked his fingers. Of course! How could he have been so stupid?

Out came the razor and he proceeded to re-cut all of my hair except the fringe. Once again he said he was finished. Once again, I pointed to my fringe and asked him to cut it. I really wished I knew the Portuguese for fringe. The same thing happened. It took me another two attempts to get him to cut my fringe. By now I wasn't far off a skinhead. Perhaps I should have gone for the Mohican.

I left Tharik's chair with my life and without a fringe, both of which states I was grateful for. Trevor saw me and burst into fits of laughter. He managed to compose himself in time to stand to attention and salute me before I returned to my chalet. He spent the rest of that day telling me about how to enrol in the Brazilian army.

That evening the team sheet went up for the first league match, at home to Luverdense the following night.

I wasn't in the squad. None of the youth teamers was in it. I was disappointed but I guess I had been expecting it. Friendlies were one thing but a league match against such a big club in the state? It wasn't going to happen. After the optimism of my debut, it was tough and didn't bode well.

Well aware that it was easy to break the curfew in our current hotel, those who were lucky enough to be selected were taken for *concentracao*. This is common practice for Brazilian teams and involves players being taken to a new hotel so that the management can attempt to monitor any partying and keep the players away from their wives and girlfriends. I wondered if the training schedule was still too tough for the King of Love Trevor to give himself enough attention.

A pleasant surprise greeted me at the game the next evening. The youth team had their first game in the under 18 Campeonato Matogrossense, which kicked-off prior to the senior team's game, also against Luverdense. We arrived just after half-time. Yago was a ball boy. My Google translate was back.

'Hey man. Just because I throw the balls back doesn't mean I'm a bad player,' he said. 'The CBF, they fuck me man. My documents, problem.' He threw his head up as a way of showing outrage at the ineptitude of the Brazilian football federation.

It turned out that he had been training with the youth team for the last week, and was due to play for them as soon as his documents were sorted. Yago's introduction to his team-mates had served as a warning from the Chairman. They had lost the previous week, and this newly assembled team was largely made up of local boys. If they dared to lose again, the Chairman had promised that he would sign 11 new boys from all over Brazil. Whatever happened, it was good to have Yago back.

Whilst those lucky enough to be selected had been in *concentracao* all day, we rejects were left to our own devices. After an early gym session I spent the day on the snooker table and in the swimming pool. It seemed that the swimming pool had followed us to the stadium. By the time the senior game was ready to kick-off the heavens had well and truly opened and soon there were patches of standing water all over the pitch.

Streams ran down the steps of the open stand. Around 800 people were tightly packed into the area covered by the roof. A few were not so lucky, and had manufactured themselves umbrellas. Some had not even done that, and were happy to get soaked to see their new team in action. Many, though, had stayed at home, content enough to watch the action on television. They certainly had enough choice of how to follow the match – there was nearly more media present than fans. The fans who were there were being geed up by Sorriso's wolf mascot, who was encouraging them to roar on their team. A chicken was strolling about the stand giving out free hats.

I missed most of the first half. Yago joined me after his stint as a ball boy, and together we spent most of it trying to get under the roof. The second half was entertaining, so Brazilian. Both teams had an attacking mentality, making the game open and fluent. All the free kicks and goal kicks were taken as short passes. There was barely a pass longer than 15 metres played in the whole half. The standard was high, the pace fast as the ball zipped about the surface as each team probed each other with captivating dribbles. Even Capone had to break into a sprint at one point. He didn't bother sprinting the next time, simply bringing the ball carrier to a halt with a blatant shirt pull. Luverdense hit the post from the resultant free kick.

Then suddenly Trevor was through one-on-one with the goalkeeper... The crowd gasped in excited anticipation as the ball left Trevor's right boot and flew past the keeper's desperate reach. The ball carried on going... and going... and going, the gasps becoming more and more excitable, the roof of the stand ready to come off, the flares ready to be released, the drums ready to be banged.

And then... silence. The net did not ripple. The ball carried on right past the post and out of play. Trevor had missed, and the crowd did not hold back on letting The King of Love know their views on his inadequacy and inability to please them. A barrage of expletives met Trevor's dejected ears. He was a *boiola, fraco, merda... fodas!*

When he was substituted a few minutes later, the crowd jeered. Now Trevor was off the pitch they could return to abusing their number one enemy: the referee. Even if he made a decision that was quite obviously correct, the whole crowd would unite in rage against him and call him and his mother every possible name. Of course, he must be a *'viado'*. Every tiny mistake prompted death threats. The only people to escape such abuse were those in the opposition's white shirts. Due to the travelling distances involved in Brazil, away fans are a rarity, meaning that the Luverdense players were largely exempt from criticism, even if they had a bigger following than most given they were from Lucas do Rio Verde 70 kilometres away. I was glad that I had made my debut in an away game. Even Capone was getting grief.

The abuse stopped only at the final whistle. The game finished 0-0, which everyone agreed was a great result considering that Luverdense had just competed in the national competition Serie C of the Campeonato Brasileiro and were the reigning champions of the Campeonato Matogrossense. It always amuses me, incidentally, when managers in England call for a winter break. In Brazil there isn't even a summer break. Football games are played all year round.

Mosca was especially happy in getting a result against his old club, a result which fuelled the Chairman's insistence that Sorriso would soon be playing at national level themselves. To get into that, a club had to win its state league or an exclusive qualification competition. With Sorriso ranked 264th, and the national system comprising the best 100, it seemed optimistic, to say the least.

Now was no time to burst the Chairman's bubble. His team had competed with one of the best in the whole state. He was almost as happy as on Christmas Eve and ordered us all to head to Andrei's father's farm after the game for supper. There, in his good mood he assured me that I would be the first choice left back the next season and that I would have a two-year professional contract. I remained focused on my poker game with Yago, though I allowed the Chairman my customary nod and smile. Pleased, he returned to his drink.

At 4am the Chairman decided that we should probably return to the hotel. He was tipsy by this point, though not giggling like a schoolgirl and still relatively sure of his movements. Eight of us jumped into his Fiat Punto, and endured a slow but bumpy journey home.

We made it home alive but that was the best that could be said of the situation I was now finding myself in. Over the next few weeks indeed, life would go from bad to worse for the youth team players as we woke up from our dream.

Mosca got no closer to knowing mine or the others' names, let alone using them. With us included, he had a squad of 34 players. SEC had no reserve team, so with seven substitutes allowed on match days, it meant that only just over half of the squad could be involved.

Even when we played matches in training the youth teamers were left on the sidelines. Do your own thing, we would be told, the implication being that if we were well behaved, we might be allowed to join in with the big boys for the last 10 minutes. Once Mosca gave me the call to join all of the best players. The initial thrill I had was soon replaced by sheer boredom, as Mosca only wanted me to be part of a wall. I spent 45 minutes jumping up and down as Alemao practiced free kick after free kick. When he finished I was dismissed back to the sidelines with the youth teamers.

Considering that the professionals focused much more on physical work and running, we rarely saw a ball. Save for *Rondos* and the odd 10 minutes of training games, we were limited to one or two technical sessions a week, which would involve practising long-range passes, headers or volleys. Occasionally I was allowed to do left back training, which was just picking the ball up, running 10 yards and shooting from the edge of the box or crossing for the strikers to score.

Other than that, it was sitting on the sidelines and waiting for the call that rarely came. It was deflating, especially after feeling I had done so well on my debut. This was foreign for some of the youth teamers, who had been used to being the best in their team throughout their fledgling football careers.

Roger couldn't take it. After just two weeks of training he had had enough. He was nice enough, but could be sullen and moody unlike most in the group and had a huge ego which took a severe hit when Rian was placed ahead of him in the pecking order. It was time to go back to his girlfriend, whose picture had followed him from the Casa dos Filtros ceiling to the ceiling above his bed in our new room. Roger's exit led to Felipe's entrance to our room.

League games came and went without a contract materialising. The night before each match, I would still have a little rush as I battled to see the teamsheet, always hopeful that my name would be there but always disappointed. We youth teamers would then ritually repair to our room where we would bad mouth Mosca and his selection. As horrible as it sounds, I would feel better if none of my peers was in the squad. Then I had the excuse that it was because I was a youth teamer that I had been overlooked.

One time, though, when Rian did make the squad, I was delighted for him and not jealous in the slightest. It was because of what I had learned from attitudes around me in this country. Training was forcing me to embrace one of the most important philosophies of Brazil: always be happy no matter what.

How could I be upset about not being included in professional training when Fernando was probably back in his corrugated iron shack living off pennies with the biggest smile on his face? No, I would have to remain positive and strong. I could not be like Roger.

20
ILL FATED

'Sefi. Problem. You, no visa. No contract. Congratulations. Problem. You...one...two...three. OK?' The Chairman had been telling me variations of this phrase for several days. He always lobbed in a few numbers randomly whenever he was struggling with his English. Whatever the message, I knew that there was a problem. By the end of the week, the Chairman assured me that no, of course there was not a problem. Why would there be as I had a two-year professional contract? Of course a new visa would be no problem. The Chairman's mixed messages disturbed me. I also wasn't having a great time with my health by now.

I had received a large parcel around the time the messages started, sent by my grandmother and containing all sorts of Christmassy decorations and foods. The only trouble was that it was now March and the parcel had been sent before Christmas. The mince pies had not been covered and the Christmas puddings were out of date and needed to be cooked in a microwave. I was so thrilled to see something that wasn't rice or a bean that I ate them straight away anyway. I love mince pies.

The next day, however, I was overwhelmed with sickness. Other players also had a bug but whereas theirs left them within a couple of days, mine remained. It got so bad that the Chairman promised to take me to the hospital. He arranged to pick me up at 11am the morning after he had assured me that a new visa would, of course, be no problem.

Naturally that meant he arrived to pick me up at 2pm. And when we finally left, it wasn't for the hospital, but for the Department of Sport and Leisure, followed by training, then the Department of Sport and Leisure once again. The purpose of the trips to the Department was to discuss my visa. After lengthy talks and much rummaging of paper with a number of different officials, it transpired that I had two options: to fly to Paraguay and then back, which would apparently get me a new visa, or simply to go home. The Chairman supported the first option, and assured me that the club would pay for the flights. Yes, the same Chairman who had assured me not even 24 hours earlier that a new visa would be 'no problem'.

Elias met me at my second visit to the Department, having been entrusted with taking me to the hospital. There was only one hospital in Sorriso, which was public, and anyone who wanted to go private faced an eight-hour trip to Cuiaba. This didn't seem excessive when contemplating the Sorriso hospital. I had not really noticed when having my medical for the youth team quite what a state it was in.

The exterior of the hospital was dirty and demoralising, with letters of its sign missing, and the place looked like it was about to fall down. All four of the ambulance's tyres were flat. I doubted the vehicle had been used for a while. The interior was no better. The walls were grey and dull and the only break in the colour was where the plaster had begun to come away from the wall. The equipment was decades old, adding to the effect that we were stuck in a black-and-white movie. The hospital was always crammed. It was small and there were many sick people in Sorriso. If you had a serious injury or illness you had to go to Cuiaba, which I suspected had an equally grim and unappealing public hospital.

'Brazil has many people,' Yago had told me back at my initial medical. 'If a few people die then so what? Brazil has many more people. This is the attitude of the government.' I hoped that the government's poorly funded establishment wasn't about to condemn me to a premature death.

Elias seemed to know everybody in the waiting room. I waited in the corner while he greeted literally everybody with a kiss on both cheeks. Even if he didn't know the recipient of the kiss he made it his task to befriend them. It was only when Elias had gone around the whole room and was content that he had spoken to everyone that I was dealt with. I was treated alongside a large woman who was regularly coughing up mucus into the rubbish bin and didn't smell great. After Elias had greeted her with his customary kisses he insisted on picking up her handbag for her and helping her out of the room after she had been diagnosed.

The doctor then moved on to me. He measured me, weighed me, tested my blood pressure and then went next door to discuss the results with a fellow professional. A new doctor came in, and he asked me some basic questions which Elias answered in dramatic style with some emphatic hand gestures. The new doctor got his stethoscope out, nodded, then gave me some tablets. I was to take four of the tablets a day over a period of five days. Then I would be fine. No premature death, and no more visits to old, crumbling hospitals.

Anderson rang that evening. He repeated his dislike for the Chairman who had told him, Anderson said, that if I stayed in Sorriso for longer than another week I would be charged for my food and accommodation and would no longer receive any wages. Who knew what was true anymore? I asked Anderson when I should book a flight home for. Three days' time came the reply. This seemed my only option.

Even if Anderson wasn't telling the truth, I had lost trust in the Chairman. He had assured me that I had a two-year professional contract. He promised me that he had sorted my visa. He had lied. His latest wheeze that I could fly to Paraguay and back, funded by the club, to get a new visa seemed fanciful. Knowing his promises I would probably end up in a Paraguayan jail.

There wasn't much point in staying in Sorriso. It had been painful watching the team from the stands every game over the last few weeks, even if they had been playing well, well enough to qualify early for the second phase with three games left. Mosca only knew Rian and Daniel Lucini's names. We were still forgotten at training. More often than not we would be left on the side to our own devices, still only being allowed to join in the last 10 minutes.

I yearned to be back at Stamford, playing in front of a supportive home crowd. No, there wasn't much good that could come out of staying. I wasn't going to get a game in the knock-out stage if I couldn't get one in a group game when we had already qualified. I'd been a professional footballer. In Brazil. That was all that I wanted to do and nobody could take it away from me. A few more weeks would have been nice, but it was not possible. I would go home. I rang Dad, who booked me a flight for a week's time.

My new team-mates began a new effort to get me to marry a Brazilian so that I could stay. By now Tangrianne was long gone, to college in Sinop, and I would not see her again. Elias said that I could marry him. I wasn't sure if he was joking. Chandler spent the whole evening trying to convince me to stay. Rian, who had obviously been learning from The King of Love, kissed me on the lips, telling me that he was much *triste* that I was leaving.

The King of Love himself gave me a much more poignant statement in English: 'Seth, you leave. I am crying for you. My eyes are crying for you. My heart is crying for you. My dick is crying for you,' said Trevor. He kissed me on the lips.

About half the team then followed him in to my chalet, all

keen to offer their condolences and ask for a commemorative picture. Ernandez looked like he might cry. We had become close. He had come into my chalet quite regularly to check up on me during my illness. Since arriving in the hotel I had spent a lot of time in his chalet, playing on his Playstation. He'd usually beat me, but it didn't matter. We were good friends.

Ernandez had taken up the role that Chandler left vacant. Like Roger, Chandler found life with the professionals hard. He was used to being the best at everything, always being the star man. Life with the professionals was a severe blow to his ego. He couldn't cope. He just went out and got drunk even more often. When he wasn't going out he was staying up until the early hours speaking with people on MSN.

More often than not, though, Chandler was breaking the curfew and heading out. Recently he had returned at 6.30am, just two hours before training. He managed to bump into just about every object in our chalet, attempted to put his hat on his head but missed, turned the television on then pointed at it and urged it to 'ssshhh', and then managed to fall over despite not colliding with anything. He didn't get up for at least five minutes.

We had grown apart. Back in Casa dos Filtros, Chandler was my best friend. He looked out for me. With the professionals it seemed that Chandler was at the centre of his own universe. Nobody else mattered. We rarely spoke anymore. He was always so tired from his night-time activities that when he wasn't training he was sleeping.

I was sure that all of the management team knew what Chandler was up to but others were being unprofessional too. The Chairman had recently given a long talk to the whole team. I wasn't sure of the exact content, but it definitely had something to do with women and SEC players coming in at 4am the day that the first team left for their previous game.

It was sad as I had shared some good times with Chandler, even recently on his better days. He was enthralled by the Christmas crackers that my grandmother had included in her parcel and was the only one who could work out how to use them. No matter how many times I urged my team-mates to pull, the cracker just slipped through their loose grasp. Chandler understood. He loved the bang that they let off. His face gave off a sense of boyish excitement as the plastic toy would fall out of the broken cracker. The crackers weren't the only source of enjoyment from the parcel. Leandro, who was still just as happy as ever and seemed unaffected by the new arrangements, wore the red Santa hat in the parcel on our Casa dos Filtros trips for a whole week. Leandro had no ego.

Chandler spent an evening trying to persuade me to stay but it felt just a token effort ahead of more pressing business for him. He invited me back to his house, told me he would miss me, asked if he could come to England, hugged me, kissed me. Then he ventured out to carnival with his friend Neyraldo, who took great pride in his long brown, blond-highlighted hair. Neyraldo, who had 'Blessed by God' tattooed in Portuguese on each forearm, was still only 23 and had been capped by Brazil as a right back at Under 21 level. He was just as much a reject as the youth-teamers, however. In a country of so many footballers, so many could fall by the wayside.

The next day everything was back to normal. Chandler was either sleeping or speaking to other people on MSN whilst sprawled out on my bed wearing my clothes. I missed the old Chandler but there was now a distance between us. It was a distance probably symbolic of how I was drifting away from the squad and the distance that would soon literally be between us.

21
GIVE AND GO

My flight home having been arranged, I met the Chairman with my Google translate Yago to tie up the loose ends before I went. Still the Chairman, his girlfriend also present at the meeting, continued with his mixed messages of congratulating me before telling me there was a problem. Bizarrely, he would then count up to five to show off his English.

Yes, there had been visa problems and I could not stay. Actually, the visa problems had surfaced a couple of weeks previously, he revealed. Technically I was an illegal immigrant. The two-year contract that the Chairman had promised? There had never been one. I was merely registered, and to play in the league just this current season.

All this came afterwards from Yago. During the meeting, I did the usual of nodding and smiling as the Chairman clumsily strung his random English phrases together, his girlfriend looking on admiringly, amazed at his intellect and blissfully unaware that I was clueless about what he was telling me. The Chairman seemed happy with my reaction and continued with his conflicting messages even after I told him of the date for my flight. He suggested he would be giving me a leaving present. I doubted it. It was about as likely as that two-year contract.

I was more concerned about getting back some of my possessions and set about tracking them down. Xuxa was adamant that my T-shirt had been a present. Acassio also thought that my boots were a gift. Chandler would return my camera in 'one minute'. Tharik assured me that I would get my towel and shorts back 'later, later'.

I held out the least hope from Joaquim, who gave me the same reply that he had given me every day of the last month when it came to a small netbook computer of mine: 'tomorrow'. Dad had bought me the computer to stay in touch but this was not easy in Casa dos Filtros due to the lack of wifi, and become even harder when, one week into my stay, the hard drive crashed.

Not to worry, Joaquim told me. He knew a guy. Leave it with him. The last I heard, my netbook was in Paraguay. I think this was the fourth different country Joaquim had told me it was in. Sometimes he even proudly sought me out himself to declare that I would get it back 'tomorrow'. I was never going to get my netbook back.

Retrieving my shorts was just as much a long shot. That evening I noticed Dida wearing them at dinner but I just couldn't bring myself to confront him. Dida was poor. He only owned a few vests and usually wore the training shorts Tharik gave us as casual. He was not exactly unapproachable but did not share the same openness and warmth of the others. He was quiet and kept himself to himself. Much of his free time was spent praying. Occasionally he came to the snooker table for a game. No good would come of confronting him. I could buy more shorts.

The shorts were easy enough for him to have taken. Every week we would hand Tharik our dirty clothes, and they would come back washed a couple of days later. Tharik would lay all of the clothes out on the Casa dos Filtros table for people to take at will. It was probably surprising that I had lost only those shorts. Maybe Dida had taken them by accident – he didn't seem to be malicious.

The netbook was certainly a more pressing matter, as was

the location of my wages. I still couldn't find them, and was pretty sure that they were lost. I had a vague recollection of hiding them in a letter that I received from my Grandmother, and an even vaguer recollection of throwing that letter in the bin once I had read it. I imagined the joy of a poverty-stricken family going through a rubbish dump, and the joyous looks on their faces as they pulled my letter, wages included, out of the food waste. Such an image made me smile. It would be apt. Brazil had taught me to be happy no matter what, and that everything happens for the best. Always.

Mosca knew that I was leaving but nothing changed. The youth teamers were still largely left to their own devices and I even went four days without touching a ball, making a mockery of that longed-for job title of 'professional footballer'. Eventually I was allowed to join in with a defensive exercise: along with the centre halves a ball was thrown in to me and I had to clear it as far away from the goal as possible. It was the first 'defensive' piece of training I had done since being in Brazil, and I felt terribly English as I booted the oncoming balls into orbit with all my might.

There was certainly something English about Mosca's training. I had not expected it at all. The only difference between what I experienced with Mosca and what went on at Stamford – apart from all the youth teamers being included back home – was the fluid, technical ability of the players. I struggled to come to terms with me and my fellow youth-teamers being disregarded so and with training that contained so little ball work. I am a big fan of 'disguised' running, using ball intensive activities such as 3 v 3 games to work on fitness.

At Stamford we usually started with a form of *Rondos*, though the players were much less comfortable with the ball at their feet. From there, as with Mosca, the session would go into physical work, the ball only coming out in the final 20 minutes. Mosca usually permitted a game of 40 minutes at the end of the session, though his sessions were typically around 45 minutes longer than those in Stamford.

The skill levels of the games were naturally better in Brazil but the structure of the session was little different – and this was supposed to be the best coach in the whole of Mato Grosso. Maybe this was how it was at all senior Brazilian teams, I mused. I was certainly disappointed, having initially enjoyed the youth team training of Emerson, where everything was done with the ball allowing skill, creativity and flair to be cultivated. What was strange was that in matches, Mosca loved the team to keep the ball and circulate it around the team.

Maybe it was expected by the senior stage that players were technically proficient and fitness was the prime requirement. Certainly all my team-mates were technically good, having played futsal pretty much since they could walk. Yago had told me that Brazilian players liked to play in tight spaces because of all the futsal and street football they were brought up on. Many had only begun full-scale football when they got to 10 or 11 years of age, and only been coached tactics from around the age of 13.

My last session in Brazil was a training match played at the stadium and about 100 people turned up to watch. Some came to heckle Trevor, who had become frustrated at the amount of stick he was getting in the media. The match lasted about an hour, and the youth teamers were allowed 20 whole minutes on the pitch.

As a way of sticking two fingers up at Mosca, I had the game of my life, even managing to nutmeg two people. I don't think Mosca even noticed. He was too busy making the final preparations for *concentracao*, to which the first team were whisked off immediately after training ahead of a match the following day. The Chairman approached me to tell me that

I would need to be leaving at 8am the day after tomorrow for my flight.

To my surprise, everything was returned by the day before my flight, except the money, which I conceded had gone. And the netbook, of course. Leandro insisted we track it down when we went to Casa dos Filtros for lunch and I was surprised to discover that it was not actually in Paraguay but just around the corner at a computer shop.

Leandro, accompanied by Daniel Lucini and Chandler, marched me to the shop and, after a lengthy discussion with the owner, he handed me my netbook. I didn't know if it was fixed or not, but I still appreciated their gesture. As a thank you, I gave Leandro the boots I had got back from Acassio. In fact, most of the stuff that I had spent the previous week tracking down was redistributed to my team-mates as presents.

Chandler was ecstatic to receive my plimsolls, which he saw as cool. He had previously offered me 120 Reais for them, but I had been annoyed with him over something so refused. Now, even if we were not as close these days, I saw that his friendship over my time in Brazil had been invaluable, and the award of the plimsolls was a fitting gesture.

In return I received a whole host of presents, most of which were given to provide me with warmth as England is 'cold, much cold'. It was all very touching. Leandro and Felipe both gave me a hoodie, Rian a hat and match shorts. From Chandler there was a towel bearing the logo of Internacional, his previous club. Trevor gave me a kiss.

The Chairman had promised to take me out for a celebratory supper at 9pm. Our transport for dinner at Casa dos Filtros was two hours late, meaning that I didn't finish my meal there until 8.30pm. I needn't have worried about rushing back. The Chairman was over an hour late picking me up, and when he did arrive he was accompanied by his girlfriend and Joaquim, who told me, with that jolly smile on his face, that I'd be getting my netbook tomorrow. I was starting to see why he was such good friends with the Chairman.

The Chairman drove us to one of the luncheonettes in the city centre, where we met with Joaquim's wife and daughter. Joaquim's daughter was similar to her father: round and jolly with a roaring and infectious laugh. His wife liked to listen to the pair talk, and had a smile on her lips throughout. AC Milan were playing Manchester United in the Champions League on the big screen, and the Chairman and Joaquim set about on their usual show calling all of the English players '*boiolas*', deriding Wayne Rooney for being weak and extolling the Brazilian Ronaldo as better than all of the players on the pitch combined.

The pair were temporarily silenced when Rooney leapt up to score a header, but soon changed the subject to coax me into singing an Elton John song, which they kept up until the food arrived. By now it was midnight, and I had long since accepted the fact that I would just be tired on my journey home the next morning. Then the Chairman looked up from his chocolate pizza.

'Sefi,' he said. 'Tomorrow, you no go at 8 the morning.' He clenched and unclenched his fist, I guessed to symbolise leaving. 'Now you go (clenching and unclenching of fist) at 11 the evening.' First, he added, I was to come to tomorrow's home game against Cacerense, a team from Caceres, which was the other side of Cuiaba. He smiled and returned to his pizza.

I wasn't overly surprised. Time was never certain in Brazil but rather a mere suggestion. Given the Chairman's inconsistencies, I wouldn't have been shocked if I was taken to the airport the day after my flight took off. He had arranged for me to meet Jocemar, the first coach of the new SEC women's team, in Cuiaba. Jocemar was staying in the city on business and the initial plan was to meet him and then spend the night in his hotel before flying home. Now I was being assured Jocemar would still meet me in Cuiaba, but just for a few hours.

A thought suddenly hit the Chairman, and he stopped midway through a mouthful of pizza. 'Oh, Sefi. I have you passport?' he asked. The prospect of returning home was beginning to look about as likely as that two-year contract. I hadn't seen my passport since handing it over to the Chairman in the first week of my stay. At some point Fabrice had had it for the Copa São Paulo, but who knew where it was now. Maybe I would have to stay in Brazil for the rest of my life. Even though I had been messed about so much lately, it didn't seem a bad option.

22
'ALWAYS YOU MY BROTHER'

I walked the now familiar walk with my fellow youth team rejects from the bus to the stadium one last time. Emotions welled up inside me as I prepared to witness my last game in Sorriso. I had never appreciated how beautifully the stand was carved into the hillside. Would I ever play in such a stadium again? The view of the rolling Brazilian countryside was breathtaking, and the fans... The SEC wolf mascot was whipping them into a passionate fury, and they seemed ready to jump over the fence and act as the twelfth man, roaring their team on to victory in the wolf's lair. A few stopped me to high five me as I worked my way to the back of the stand, but most were too fixed on the game.

My last couple of days had been spent as much of my time in the senior squad had been: a bout of physical work in the morning at the gym followed by snooker, swimming, and video games in Ernandez's room. The physical work had certainly had an effect on me. My first time in the gym I was clueless. Yago had to teach me how to do all of the weights, even those as simple as bicep curls.

After months of work my arms no longer resembled two pale twigs. The sun had bronzed them and the repetitive lifting had even given me a bit of definition. I had gone to Brazil weighing a measly 67 kilogrammes and might have been expected to lose weight, what with all the running and the heat. Instead, thanks to the weights, I was now a more muscular 69 kilos, 10 stones 8 lbs. My resting heart rate had gone down to 51. I had never been so fit in my life and, in addition to the exposure to Brazilian football I enjoyed, I had never felt so assured on the pitch. It was just a shame that I had spent so little time recently on this pitch I now looked out on.

This final game suddenly put everything into perspective for me. I began to see just how good my team-mates were. The way they moved the ball, their skill, their technique, their flair, it was just so superior to anything I had ever been involved with. It was artistry. It was inspired. It was genius. I had been lucky in being invited to Brazil in the first place, but to be a part of such a team... well, that was special.

Being honest with myself, now I realised why Mosca hadn't bothered to learn my name, hurtful as it was. There was no way I could ever be as competent on the pitch as these men in green and white. They had been expected to qualify from their group this season but few expected them to be top of the league, having won every home game so far after the opening draw with Luverdense, if only by a single goal each time. Beating Sinop away was the big result for the fans, as with derbies everywhere, and they still had the home game to enjoy.

My frustration had been the result of youthful exuberance. I was too busy channelling all of my energy into a desire to play that I had never stepped back to see the bigger picture. I suppose it was the folly, or the blinkered naivety, of youth. Instead of being bitter I sat back, and let the 11 men entertain me.

Barely 10 minutes had passed when SEC scored their first goal. Alemao's corner was whipped in and carried on going right into the stanchion of the goal. Leo Rosa soon doubled the lead, and SEC's dominance was only furthered when the referee produced a soft red card for a Cacerense player after a tackle which would have been considered a good challenge in England.

Sorriso continued to move the ball with remarkable speed. Their one-touch football was a joy. Even Trevor was escaping his usual abuse. As the second half went on, however, SEC eased up and Cacerense came back into the game, reducing the arrears following a long ball into the penalty area.

A few SEC fans clapped sarcastically, the rest vented their anger. They were finally appeased five minutes from time when Capone scored a free kick from 35 yards out, the ball flying into the net via the crossbar, to make it 3-1. The crowd erupted. The 11 home players lost it, running wildly and jumping onto the fence that separated them from the fans. Firecrackers and flares filled the night sky. Drums were beaten. People danced.

How to equate the standard with England? Though not ranked highly enough for the national leagues, Sorriso could probably be seen as similar in status to a Conference club, with so many professional set-ups in Brazil. The standard was so much higher than our non-League, however, and more akin to League Two or the lower reaches of League One. There were players such as Capone, Leonardo – who was still in his early 30s – and Alemao who had played at the highest level. There was also Neyraldo who was representing his country at youth level just two years earlier but was nowhere near the team.

Rather than head straight to the bus station, the Chairman convinced me to go for a dinner of cold rice and beans at Casa dos Filtros with the rest of the team. It seemed an appropriate send-off. The time was 10.15p.m. – 45 minutes before the Chairman had said I would leave. After wolfing down my unappetising meal, the Chairman assured me that everything was still going to plan, looking surprised when I questioned him.

'Ah, no. You with trainerdore Mosca,' he said. Considering that he had earlier handed me a bus ticket worth 75 Reais, his latest statement confused me. The new arrangement was that Mosca would drive me to Cuiaba as he had business to attend to. When I asked what time I would leave, the Chairman told me 'eleven hours'.

By now the time was 11.10pm. I did not have any of my luggage and still had not seen my passport. I did my customary nodding and smiling with the Chairman, trying not to let the sheer panic I was feeling inside show.

There was no sign of Mosca when the bus arrived at Casa dos Filtros to take us back to our hotel. I had one final look around the place, my eyes lingering on the window with the missing bar. I could almost hear Leo's squeals as he jumped head first through that window covered in blood. I could feel Oswaldo shaking my feet in the morning. I could taste the salt from the sweat that ran down my face. They were the memories of a lifetime. Memories of a life that seemed far superior to anything else that I had so far lived. Casa dos Filtros was more than a home. It was special. It had defined me.

Mosca wasn't back at the hotel either. I packed quickly and showered. Most of my stuff had found its way back into my case, and other than my wages and passport I wasn't missing anything important. The Chairman came calling at 10 to midnight.

'*Bora bora* Sefi. Let's go, let's go! *Vamos!*' he urged. I wasn't going with Mosca after all. The Chairman would take me to the bus station; my bus would leave at 12.40am. I stepped into the Chairman's small rusty Fiat Punto clutching my three new Sorriso match shirts which had been given to me as presents. 'For your mother, father and you,' Tharik had told me.

'*Fome?*' the Chairman asked. I told him I wasn't hungry, but he insisted on taking me out for more supper at a luncheon-ette with Capone and all of his family anyway. The concept of time to me and the Chairman were very different. The supper itself was pleasant – Capone's family were all warm-hearted and keen to share jokes with me – and I'm sure that I would have enjoyed it greatly had I not been worried about making it back to England.

Finally, at 12.37am, the Chairman decided it was time to go to the bus station. The goodbyes weren't overly emotional. As he had apparently done to everyone else, the Chairman assured Capone and his family that he had held extensive talks with me and that I would be returning to Sorriso in a couple of weeks. I smiled and nodded, and set about hugging everyone around the table.

Oblivious to time, the Chairmen presented me with some more presents in his car: a boot bag, two packets of coffee, bizarrely a match shirt from '*Gigante do Norte*' – a football team of midgets from the North of Brazil – two pairs of SEC match shorts and a pair of training shorts. He gave the kind of look that a father gives a son, then put his hand on my shoulder. His mouth curved into a smile, a smile which reeked of pride. It was impossible not to smile back. Satisfied with his work, the Chairman turned back to face the road and started the car.

We reached the bus station at 12.48am just as the bus was pulling away – surprisingly just eight minutes late. Suddenly the Chairman burst into action. He swerved into the path of the bus, slammed on his handbrake and leapt out of the car, raising his hand in front of the oncoming bus. I sat there stunned, all the while feeling like I was in Tiananmen Square. The bus driver was equally stunned at the sight of this pot-bellied man leaping out of his tiny vehicle and demanding that he stop. He obeyed the Chairman's request, bringing the bus to a standstill.

Pleased with his work, the Chairman retrieved my luggage from the boot of his car before handing my ticket to the bus driver. The driver approved it and signalled for me to put my luggage into the storage. I turned to the Chairman, trying but failing to choke back my emotions. He stood there, his arms open. We embraced.

'Always you my brother,' he whispered in my ear. I knew that, for once, he was being genuine. He truly meant it.

'Ah!' he added. He had almost forgotten and so had I. He reached into his back pocket and handed me my passport. We hugged once more and then that was it. I got on to the bus and we rolled out of the station. The experience was over for now but the lessons and the legacy would last. It felt like I would be back one day. Less *Adeus Sorriso*, more *Ate logo* – See you later.

23
DEPARTURE DRAMAS

The bus journey went smoothly, metaphorically if not physically. Sleep proved challenging as we travelled through the night over dirt roads full of potholes, but I was too afraid to take my eyes off my luggage anyway. The bus was full with I knew not what kind of stranger in the dark. We arrived in Cuiaba at 8.45am and, just as the Chairman had promised, Jocemar turned up at exactly 9 o'clock to pick me up. I had finally met a Brazilian with a concept of time. I hauled my luggage into the back of Jocemar's sports car and he took me to his hotel.

Once there, Jocemar left me. He had business to attend to and would be back at midday. There was no rush. My flight was not till the afternoon and I could shower and sleep, as well as eat the breakfast he had prepared for me. All three were highly appealing. A warm shower had been rare, and this one provided more than just a dribble of water while the food of croissant, grapes and yoghurt was luxurious by comparison with that staple diet in Sorriso of rice, beans, crusty rolls and sour milkshake. I crashed contentedly on to the double bed to sleep.

I was awoken by Jocemar's return. He had booked a taxi that would take me to the airport for 1pm and until then we could talk. He asked me for my impressions of Sorriso, what I had enjoyed and what I didn't. He told me more about SEC, that they had a wage bill of 50,000 Reais a month. For a small Brazilian team this was sizeable but small when compared to Mixto's, which was 300,000 Reais a month. Mixto were from

Cuiaba, their name coming from their origins as a team of different races, and were a big club who had played in Serie A. They were currently doing poorly in the other group from SEC in the Campeonato Matogrossense, which they had won many times.

Jocemar, a short, plump and jolly man of about 40, was enjoying being the head coach of the SEC women's team, he said. The girls were very skilful, much more skilful than anyone from England, he insisted. He had recently taken an under 13 side to Cuiaba for a tournament which they had won, and was clearly proud of it.

The horn of the waiting taxi interrupted our conversation. We embraced, and Jocemar promised to stay in touch. I set off for Cuiaba airport and arrived over an hour before I was due to take off for my internal flight to Brasilia. The nerves I had been feeling about the journey home began to subside once I breezed through airport security. The security staff found my suggestion that I remove my liquids from my luggage laughable. Of course there wouldn't be a terrorist in Cuiaba! No, I could go straight through.

My journey proceeded just as smoothly once I arrived in Brasilia. I had five hours until my flight to London, and again I managed to steam through security. I now decided I had better sort out my suitcase. It had holes in it and the gaffer tape I had used to patch them up was peeling off. Thankfully, airport staff wrapped my suitcase in cling film and I retreated to a comfy looking chair and fell into a light sleep. I dozed in and out of consciousness until there were two hours left to my flight. This gave me plenty of time to browse the shops and buy gifts for my friends and family.

I recalled the last time I had been at this airport on my way to Sorriso when I suddenly felt alone and so young. Now I felt a boy no longer. Now I felt in control. I had come a long way, I thought, and not just literally. Things do have a habit of turning on you in Brazil just when you think things are going to plan, however.

Then again, they probably would in many countries when you no longer have a valid visa.

The whole visa issue had slipped out of my mind, what with everything going so smoothly so far. That was until I smugly decided to go through customs and wait the final hour for my flight at the gate. I presented my passport to the woman at customs and she scanned it on her machine. The gate didn't open. She called a colleague. Together they looked at my passport, looked at the machine, then looked back at my passport, all the while speaking in hushed tones. My heart was racing, my previous cool gone. All I could think of was Brazilian prisons. Would I get my own cell? Would there be rats? How long would they lock me up for? Would I ever get back to England? Would I ever see my family again?

After what seemed a lifetime, but in reality was no more than a minute or so, the woman on the gate slowly looked up and beckoned me to come closer. She pointed at my passport, then at her machine.

'You. Problem,' she said. I had grown sick of hearing that word over the last month. Her colleague had already called an armed policeman, and I was to follow him. I didn't know what was happening. I was scared. All I knew was that my flight was straight on and I was going away from it. I followed the police-man back through the shops and down a maze of corridors and stairs until we arrived at a dark underground office. There were several more policemen here, and the armed policeman motioned towards a seat at the desk of a large lady in police uniform. I sat obediently.

I had seen hundreds of films like this: the bad guy going down under ground for interrogation, the police not satisfied with his answers. The torture. The abuse. I looked at my tor-mentor across the desk. She didn't look like she was about to torture me, to be fair, even if my imagination was racing. And even if she was, I doubted that she was in a good enough physical shape to hurt me. Neither did her face suggest that she was about to break into a rage over what terrible atrocities I had committed in her country. The only look she wore was one of mild boredom. I was still petrified. Suddenly feeling cold, I would have given anything to be back home, spread across my sofa with the heating on and my family surrounding me. Home was safety.

'Why are you still in Brazil?' she asked in good English. I noticed that an armed policeman had moved himself within my eyeline – a warning. I garbled frantically about how I had been a professional footballer and how the Chairman had misled me and how I was told I had a two-year contract but then this wasn't true and I had to get a new visa after it had run out and how I had only been given my passport back the previous night anyway and I was really sorry but I couldn't help it.

I was exhausted by the time I finished my final sentence and slouched back in my chair. The large woman continued to stare at me. Maybe I had been too dramatic. I had spoken so quickly that she probably only caught a fraction of what I had said. Her look of mild boredom had been replaced with a look of moderate interest.

'Where is your tourist slip?' she asked. Her tone was emo-tionless, machine-like. I hadn't seen my tourist slip since I first arrived in Brasilia. Everyone on the plane had been made to fill one out so that they could enter Brazil. I think I threw it away once I got to Casa dos Filtros. I shrugged at her.

'I'm sorry. I don't know,' I blurted out. She continued to stare at me. She called over two other women in police uniform and my immediate future was once again discussed in hushed tones. I was now sure that I would be going to prison. I just hoped that they'd let me off lightly. Just a few years then back to England. It wouldn't be the end of the world. I'd still just about be clinging on to my youth by the time I got home. I could still make something of myself. Go to university, maybe get a good job. I'd just have to endure whatever I was presented with.

The women finished their huddle and the large one returned to face me. I couldn't read her face. She gave away no clues.

'Mr Burkett, you have been in Brazil illegally for nine days. Your visa is not valid. That is why you were brought here,' she said. 'You do not have a tourist slip either. Failure to show a tourist slip can result in a 500 Reais fine.' She spoke in the factual, monotone voice of a judge condemning a guilty man.

'We understand that you are young. There have been mistakes,' she added. She passed on to me a letter a colleague had just handed her. 'This time, we forget the tourist slip. We are issuing you with a fine for not having a valid visa. You may go home, but until you pay this fine, you are not allowed to return to Brazil.'

I looked down at my official letter. My heart leapt. I was free. I would be going home. And for my terrible atrocity, the price they were demanding for me being an illegal immigrant was just 52 Reais should I wish to come back to the country in the future. I wasn't going to prison. I wanted to jump over that desk and hug and kiss the large woman. I wanted to high-five all of the armed policeman and lead them in a samba. I didn't. I just went into my default position of nodding and smiling and followed a policeman safely back through customs. He grimaced as I left him, as if to warn me not to enter Brazil again.

I reached the gate five minutes before the scheduled take-off time, but there were still plenty more people to arrive yet in the departure lounge. I had put so much emotional effort into my ordeal with the police that I had almost forgotten that I was struggling to make the flight. Relief flooded over me even before I stepped on to that plane, which considering my previous few weeks was foolish. Nothing was ever certain until it happened.

Fortunately I made it on to the plane and calmed down and stopped sweating. And started contemplating the life I had been living over the past season, asking myself in particular one question: just why is Brazil the best footballing nation on earth?

I always thought that England was passionate about the sport but Brazil is obsessional. There are football pitches everywhere, and at weekends there are games on every single one. Every evening you see small children walking home barefoot with a ball tucked under their arm. There is football on the television every day with every shop and bar showing it. The sport is a massive advertising vehicle for products that have nothing to do with the game and is always used in any type of tourism advert. This is a nation so obsessed that when I was there, children were using physics lessons to work out precisely how a Palmeiras player, Diego Souza, scored a wonder volley from the halfway line without breaking stride and how it didn't bounce until it was in the net.

In Brazil, I saw players aged 13 and older train twice during the day and spend their evenings at night school. Add this to being far away from home in a different state for up to six months at a time and that is commitment. When I was playing for Northampton at the age of 13 I had to train twice a week and play on a Sunday. That was five and a half hours of contact time in a week. Most Brazilian 13-year-olds have received more than that before Wednesday each week.

Maybe the answer also lies in how structured football is in each nation. Structure is deemed highly important in England.

Often the sessions are so structured that the players will be encouraged not to think for themselves and the coach, eager to make it look like he is doing something, is only too happy to tell the player what they should be doing. Consequently the player does not learn properly to think for himself and he builds up an over-reliance on his coach.

Growing up, fewer and fewer English players are learning their trade in the streets. My old coach at Northampton, Kristian Heames, set up his own academy system shortly after I was released from the club. Kristian was one of the few coaches who cultivated and encouraged creativity and flair in his players. One week he would get his centre half to play on the wing, the next he would make him play in goal. Winning did not matter to Kristian. He wanted the players to try their flicks and tricks without fear.

At first the players at his academy were not allowed to play for a Sunday league side, only for Kristian's academy. As the years went on, Kristian realised that the ability of the new influxes of players was decreasing, however. They no longer had a command of the most basic requirements of tackling, passing, shooting and dribbling. It was Kristian's belief that English propaganda, where every stranger is a paedophile and every car signals danger, had confined children to their homes. Their parents were only too happy to have them playing video games upstairs.

Many schools don't even allow children to play football at lunchtimes or break times anymore. A child walking through the streets with a football tucked under their arm is now a rare sight. Eventually Kristian conceded defeat, and told his players that they needed to be playing more. He let them play for their Sunday league teams, all the while bemoaning the sorry state of English football.

In addition, individual talent is encouraged in Brazil –

nutmegs are celebrated, stepovers are plenty and the beating of an opponent when one-on-one is applauded. Such traits are regarded in England as 'showing off'. Attitudes of crowds are different too. I recall watching an English game on television and seeing a central midfield player losing the ball on the half-way line after a poor touch. His next action was to perform a crunching slide tackle and concede a throw-in. The crowd applauded and some sang his name. Such a thing – somebody being cheered for essentially losing possession – would never happen in Brazil.

It had been a true pleasure to play the Brazilian way, even if I had appeared to them to be that Englishman losing posses-sion at times. Now a remarkable episode in my life was over. My relationship with Brazil was not, however.

24
THE FAMILY TRAILBLAZER

Mum could not get any words out. She just ran up and hugged me, her eyes streaming with tears. She had her Sethy boy back. After what seemed an eternity, she finally released me from her grip, tears still falling down her face. Now it was Dad's turn. He simply put his hand on my shoulder and smiled. 'It's good to have you back, son. The whole family is so proud of you,' he said. I felt a surge of joy. I hadn't realised just how much I had missed them.

My first few weeks back home were great: food, friends, family. Safety. I returned to my comfortable middle-class existence and life was easy. After a while, though, the novelty began to wear off as I realised there was little to do and I was on my own. My friends went back to university, my parents went out to work all day and my sister was at school.

I couldn't even play football. I needed international clearance to play for any team in England, which meant that the CBF had to inform the FA that I was not under any bans. I hadn't applied for clearance mainly because it would be at least 30 days before I could play, taking me virtually to the end of the season in England, and Anderson had told me that there was a club in the São Paulo state league – Taboao do Serra – interested in signing me. It seemed unlikely but strange things had already happened. I just practiced and practiced in my garden, going over all of the footwork exercises that Emerson had given me. I had to stay fresh.

With time on my hands, I began to look more into the story of my great grandfather's brother – my great great uncle – Charlie Williams. My grandparents, who had never been interested in football and who were prone to exaggeration, had spoken of him being Arsenal's first goalkeeper and before I went to Brazil, Dad had gone to Dan Brennan, who wrote for Arsenal magazine, to see if they were right.

Sure enough, Dan said after checking it out, Charlie Williams had been Arsenal's first professional goalkeeper, shortly before the turn of the 20th century. Indeed the family connection to the club was strong. Charlie's sister had married a man named Joseph Smith, whose father, also named Joseph Smith, was one of the core group of workers at the Royal Arsenal armaments factory in Dial Square, Woolwich who decided in 1886 that they should create a football team. It was Smith who went around the factory with a top hat, urging the workers to donate sixpence so they could buy a football. It was Smith who unsuccessfully negotiated with Plumstead Cricket Club for the use of their facilities for home matches. And it was Smith who introduced Charlie to Dial Square, the first name of the team before it soon became Royal Arsenal.

The workers would spend each Sunday afternoon on Plumstead Common in South East London, practising their skills. When Charlie was just a teenager, Smith brought him along. Charlie was familiar to many of the workers – he had occasionally worked in the factory as a moulder, and his family was well known within the workshops. His lankiness, along with his age, led to him being placed in goal and he proved hard to beat.

Accounts had it that his great span made him especially adept at dealing with crosses and he had a raw power and an ability to leap and stop the shots of the physically developed men he played alongside. He was on the books of a Kent team, Erith and when they turned up to play a Royal Arsenal side without a goalkeeper Charlie was volunteered to fill in. He did a good job, his performance impressing the Royal Arsenal players enough for them to begin involving him in their games.

Charlie made his Royal Arsenal debut against Nottingham Forest in 1891, aged 18, and by the 1893/94 season was established as first-choice goalkeeper, which was good timing for him. That season they turned professional, became Woolwich Arsenal and were accepted as the first southern club in the Football League, entering the Second Division.

He duly took his place in goal for Woolwich Arsenal's very first professional game, against Newcastle United on September 2nd, 1893. He must soon have begun to doubt the honour bestowed upon him, however, as he was in the firing line for some of Arsenal's heaviest defeats that season, including a 0-6 loss to Newcastle United and a 0-5 loss to Liverpool. The potential that Charlie had shown on Plumstead Common was disregarded at the end of the season when Arsenal signed a new goalkeeper, Harry Storer.

Fortunately for Charlie, his performances had been good enough to interest a new suitor in Manchester City, who had been newly formed for the 1894-95 season, and he was signed along with a figure who would become one of the greatest of the English game, playing for both City and United and helping to found the Professional Footballers' Association – Billy Meredith.

Together they proved a success, and grew to become good friends. Manchester City were soon promoted to the First Division, and the crowds began flocking in. And in City's inaugural season in the top flight, Charlie created a moment of history. Nobody knew whether he meant it – he himself insisted that he did – but on April 14, 1900, Charlie Williams entered the record books as the first goalkeeper to score from a goal clearance. His long, wind-assisted drop-kick caught out Sunderland's goalkeeper Teddy Doig, the ball bouncing three times before twisting out of Doig's reach and nestling in the back of the net. Doig, in an attempt to avoid ridicule, claimed that he had been inspecting a damaged finger and was caught unawares by Charlie's speculative effort.

After eight years in Manchester, Charlie returned to London. He signed for Tottenham Hotspur as a back-up 'keeper, and had to make do with the majority of his appearances coming in the Tottenham reserve team. One was against the reserve side of his old employers Woolwich Arsenal and unfortunately the Arsenal supporters who congregated behind Charlie's goal did not remember him too fondly. The same supporters had forced his replacement, Harry Storer, out of the club after just two seasons and Harry left complaining of the disgraceful and unfair manner in which the crowd had behaved, insisting that he was unable to perform to the best of his abilities under the constant booing and hooting.

The guilty section of supporters had not taken any notice of Harry's complaints, and proved to be just as disgraceful and unfair towards Charlie, according to legend. Heckles and jibes cut through the cold air. Charlie was jeered, insulted and ridiculed. Eventually he could take no more. After hearing one particularly foul-mouthed comment, he turned around to find the perpetrator. He marched into the crowd, grabbed the miscreant by the scruff of his neck and thumped him. His point proven, and his victim decidedly dazed, Charlie returned to his goal to see out the rest of the game.

It proved to be the beginning of the end for him, though. Tottenham suspended him and soon offloaded him to Norwich City, where he remained for a short time before retiring while at Brentford. As an interesting addendum, Dan told us, Charlie had been manager of the Denmark national team at the Olympic Games in London in 1908.

All this I found out from Dan – who subsequently invited my grandparents to the Emirates to watch Arsenal – the summer before I went to Sorriso. Now I contacted him again to see if he could tell me any more about Charlie perhaps having gone to Brazil. My grandparents had mentioned it, but were less sure about this. What I discovered was a revelation and an echo of my own journey.

Family history had it that Charlie became something of a black sheep. First they perceived that he had darkened the family name and seriously damaged his earning potential with his promiscuity and subsequent impregnation of a girl when he was just 20. Charlie's mother ensured that he married the girl pretty soon after the child was conceived, but the damage had already been done.

Second, Charlie had estranged himself by refusing to share his earnings with his hard-up family. It was certainly no secret that Charlie had a great deal of money. In 1898 he had shared a benefit of £75 with his close friend Billy Meredith, and his salary had not been ungenerous. The final straw was when Charlie, who had divorced his wife in 1910 – yet another source of shame upon them and reason to shun him – brought a 'hussy' home and introduced her to the family. My grandparents thought the woman was from Brazil, where Charlie had been, but they were not sure.

To my surprise and delight, Dan came back to me to confirm the Brazil link – and much, much more. Charlie had not only gone to Brazil, but he had played an integral part in their football history.

Following his retirement from the game, Charlie joined the French club OSC Lille as manager. From there he joined Danish side B93, and his subsequent success led to him being appointed manager of the Danish team for the 1908 Olympics. They impressed, cruising to the final after beating France B 9-0 and France A 17-1, with Sophus Nielsen scoring a remarkable ten goals in the second game.

Such was France A's embarrassment at their thrashing that they refused to play in the bronze medal match. The Danes, however, were buoyed and took a great deal of confidence into their gold medal match against Great Britain. Sadly for Charlie, although they managed to compete for large parts of the game, Nielsen could not repeat his magic from the semi-final and Great Britain won 2-0. The fact that the Danes were not humbled by their then mighty opponents was testimony to the techniques of their English coach, though, and Charlie's reputation was enhanced around the world of football.

One team who had taken particular note of Charlie's achievements was Fluminese Futebol Clube. Founded in 1902 by Oscar Cox, they had enjoyed early success. Based in the Laranjeiras district of Rio de Janeiro, the team comprised the sons of the Rio elite. Many of them, such as Oscar, a Brazilian whose father was an English diplomat, had first experienced football whilst studying in Europe and developed a passion for the sport. Because of the make-up of the team, Fluminese maintained a close link with the aristocracy, and the club was seen as a plaything of the rich.

They enjoyed great success. After winning their first ever match 8-0 against Rio FC, they won the Rio state league in 1906, 1907, 1908 and 1909. The 1909 league title was a sore point for Fluminese, however, as they were forced to share it with their rivals, Botafogo. Matters worsened in 1910 when they failed to win the title and, seeking expert guidance to return the title to Laranjeiras, Fluminese sent a delegation of club officials to England.

They sought out Charlie Williams and told him that they wanted him to win the league title for Fluminese. They gave him an unprecedented offer of £18 pounds a month, plus room, board and two round trip tickets between Brazil and England. Such faith in his abilities – he was the first ever professional coach to be offered a long-term contract by a Brazilian club – convinced him and he accepted the delegation's request to become Fluminese's new manager.

Upon his arrival in Rio, Charlie was met by an inquisitive squad. They were intrigued by this so-called expert coach who had had immense success in Europe. All very well they thought, but could he replicate it in such a different environment? He certainly could. Charlie led Fluminese to the Rio state league title in his first year, 1911.

The club's joy did not last long into the following season, however. Despite how emphatically Fluminese had beaten their first six opponents with Charlie as manager – scoring 20 goals and conceding just one – there were problems in the camp, due to a fractured relationship between the board and players, possibly due to money. The problems became so bad that nine of the 11 first-team players defected to set up a team who would go on to be one of Brazil's most celebrated.

Before then, Flamengo had exclusively been a rowing club. The nine dissatisfied players made their home there because one of their number, Alberto Borghert, who had been Charlie's captain at Fluminese, rowed for Flamengo. The club was officially formed on Christmas Eve in 1911 and the players began training on the local beach. The locals soon took an interest in the players' new project and gave them ardent support, the different approaches of the two clubs creating the rivalry between Fluminense and Flamengo that still exists, bitterly, to this day.

Fluminese, traditionally associated with the elite of Rio society, trained far away from prying eyes. In contrast, Flamengo trained fully in the public gaze, and their interaction with the local people soon led to the perception that Flamengo was the club of the working class. The nine founders easily found players to make up the team and they played their first ever game in May 1912 beating Mangueira 16-2.

Charlie had been monitoring the rise of Flamengo closely. His initial outrage was now replaced by a sense of foreboding that Fluminese's reign was about to come under serious threat, especially considering his now threadbare squad. The newly formed Flamengo side had been accepted into the Rio state league for 1912 and were aiming to take Fluminese's crown. Their friendly results suggested that they just might and when they began the season well, brushing aside all competition, Charlie's concerns were shown to be well founded.

Fluminense, too, had started the season well, however and when the two clubs met for the first ever time on July the seventh, both were unbeaten. It was a meeting that would mark the beginning of one of the fiercest rivalries in World football: the 'Fla-Flu' derby.

Charlie led his team out to face their rivals and, in gentle-manly fashion, stopped to shake the hands of the men who had deserted him before heading toward the touchline. The Fluminense board of directors, by contrast, would go nowhere near these 'traitors' and headed straight for the stands, which were occupied by an intrigued audience of 800 people – a fairly respectable number for the time.

They were treated to an intense battle. The Flamengo team were skilled, and training on the beach had done wonders for their stamina, but Charlie had whipped his team into a formida-ble outfit. It swung this way and that, the score standing at 2-2 as the game entered its final 15 minutes. Then Bartho struck what would prove to be the winner for Fluminense. At the final whistle, he was mobbed by his ecstatic team-mates.

The aristocrats had proved their superiority. In the words of one Brazilian commentator the win represented 'the victory that could never be avenged'. Fluminense did not win the title that year. They didn't even finish runners-up. But none of that mattered. The fact that Flamengo finished in the runner-up spot did not even bother many Fluminese fans. The 3-2 victory counted for so much more.

Charlie left Brazil at the end of the season and returned to London. It seems that it was at this point that the 'hussy' was introduced to the family, resulting in Charlie's ostracism. Outcast from the family, he attempted to build a new life in England but he just could not recapture the excitement of Brazil. Also, his 'hussy' girlfriend was missing the warmth of her country and just couldn't adapt to the English food. She yearned for a bowl of her favourite *feijoada*.

When Fluminese once again came calling, Charlie and his girlfriend jumped at the chance. Nearly a decade had gone by since he had left Brazil, but his coaching talents had not been forgotten. Charlie once again led Fluminese to the Rio state title in 1924. He repeated the feat in 1928, this time with a different Rio club – America FC – with an impressive record of 18 victories and just one defeat. The following year, he even won another Rio title with his third club, Botafogo.

When Charlie finally retired from football in 1934, he decided that Brazil was now his home and he lived out his years there until his death in 1952, at the age of 79. He had found it easier to sever his relationship with his family in England than with the country and the life he had become attached to. Charlie was survived by his son, Charles Williams, who served as a top-flight referee in the Brazilian leagues in the 1950s.

Charlie's story fascinated me, even filled me with awe. I began to wish I had known about it about it before going to Brazil. It might have been a comfort at some times, a boost at others, to know that someone in my family had gone through something akin to what I was experiencing.

But, then I thought it through. We each have our own paths

to take and nothing could really have improved my Sorriso experience. Charlie took his path as a mature man at the end of
his football career. Mine was as a youth, with so much still to
experience. If not similar personalities by the sound of it, we
both had in common an adventure to a country we came to
love and like him I had found the courage within myself to do
something that could have been a disaster but was ultimately
successful. Something in my background, my genes, my soul,
must have been taking me to the place of one of my ancestors.

I would have liked to have known Charlie Williams. I would
like to find and get to know his descendants. Perhaps I will
one day.

25
FROM FUTEBOL TO FUTSAL

The season in England petered out. Stamford missed out on the play-offs. I went to watch them a few times, but the frustration was difficult to bear. I wanted to be out there playing. By then, Sorriso's challenge in the Campeonato Matogrossense had long since evaporated. They had reached the second stage quite comfortably, winning their qualification group by a point with Luverdense as runners-up. SEC even beat Caceres 14-0 in their penultimate game. Rian made the substitutes' bench but none of the other youth teamers was involved.

The win must have given SEC false confidence. Despite playing the fourth-placed team, Araguaia, from the other qualification group, Sorriso crashed out of the seeded quarter-finals 6-3 on aggregate. I had barely missed anything by going home early. I was glad that I had not listened to the Chairman and gone to Paraguay and back. Everything truly does happen for the best.

My move to Taboao do Serra fell through, unsurprisingly. Apparently they had run out of money and couldn't afford me. I told Anderson that I didn't care about money, that I just wanted to go back to Brazil and play. He said this wasn't an option, however. I was disappointed but imbued now with that philosophy I had acquired in Sorriso: this had happened for a reason. I would go to university as all of my family had. Loughborough still had a place for me to do English and Sports Science and I would take it up. Then maybe after the three years

I could chance my luck in Brazil once more.

To keep fit, I began to play futsal. Anderson had joined with my old manager at the Stamford youth team, Guy Walton, to set up a team in the name of Stamford. Other than Guy's son, Jake, the team was made up of Brazilians. I took to the game immediately. I had been introduced to it as a nine-year-old in the Peterborough United academy by an innovative coach called Kit Carson, who was then supported in his role by Dan Ashworth, now director of elite development at the FA. Many good coaches recognised it as an effective developmental tool for the outdoor game, and the Brazilian style of play that I had experienced in Sorriso was shaped by the sport.

In fact, the game was first developed in Brazil, with Uruguay also at the vanguard, in the 1930s and 40s and has had a huge impact on the style of football in South America. The game comprises two teams of five players but unlike traditional five-a-side, there is no rule against the ball going above head height. Players can go anywhere on the court and the ball can go out of play. The ball is slightly smaller than a size four but is heavier, placing emphasis on individual skill, technical proficiency and fast movement in tight spaces.

After a few games for Stamford, Loughborough University came calling and it would be ideal as I was going to study there. They had a team who played in the National Futsal League, and their manager Michael Skubala was the assistant coach of England. They wanted me and Jake to sign for them.

The CBF still hadn't authorised my international clearance, but enough time had now passed for me to be eligible to play in England once again. I scored a hat-trick for Loughborough on my debut in an 11-1 victory against Hereford. I could feel that this was the start of something special. Quickly I bought into the vision of the game as outlined by 'Skubes', as we called the manager.

Even if he didn't see futsal as the main reason for the superior development of young Brazilian players, just one of many factors, Skubes pointed to a player having 33 per cent more touches in futsal than football, which was important to keep youngsters involved in the game. A futsal player, he added, needed to make quick, skilful and instinctive decisions in milliseconds. Decision making is vital, as is the ability to play under the pressure of an opponent due to the confined spaces.

Anderson was impressed with my new-found ability on the futsal court, rekindling his interest in giving me one final shot at playing professional football. This was typical of him. There is a perception of football agents that they are greedy, only looking out for themselves and only interested in money. That was not Anderson. I'm not sure I have ever met a more caring person. He never asked me for a penny of my wages in Brazil and was always concerned for my welfare. Yes, he made decent money from Denilson, but quite often he would be funding players himself as as they chased their dreams.

He had grouped together a team of his imports to play in a trial game in Croydon, which would be watched by a number of scouts. By this stage I wasn't too fussed. I was preparing myself to go to Loughborough and the respect I had earned so quickly in the futsal team made me believe that it was going to be an easy transition.

Still, a return to Brazil was the only way that I would give up my education for professional football, so nothing ventured, nothing gained... Thus did I embark on a bizarre journey to South London and back in my small Ford Fiesta with a bunch of Brazilians that would go via an Accident and Emergency unit. And which would take in the home of an Arsenal footballer and encounter some high-class prostitutes on the way.

While I was blase about the whole day, for Miguel it was a big opportunity. Anderson had spotted him five years ago playing in a modest professional side in São Paulo and brought him over to Europe. It was the childhood dream of a Brazilian player. Europe is where the money is. Miguel was pleased that I had enjoyed Brazil, but he did not understand why I wanted to play there. Why play in Brazil when I could stay in Europe with all its money? He just didn't understand the lure of Brazil to everyone outside of South America.

Miguel had enjoyed initial success in Europe. He trialled at Milton Keynes Dons before Anderson got him a contract with a German fourth division team, TSV Torgelow. He did well with them. Miguel was a striker, and he endeared himself to their small but loyal band of fans by scoring some important goals. Life was good - until a late tackle resulted in a broken leg. Suddenly he was alone and isolated in a foreign country. He came back to live with Anderson while he recovered.

Sadly, when he was finally able to play again he was not quite the same player. It would take some time. The German club were not financially powerful and said they could not pay him while they waited for him to get back to his best form. Since then, Miguel had been back at Anderson's, learning English and studying at Stamford College, all the while waiting for his big opportunity.

On the journey down to South London, we sang *Chora me Liga* together. He was impressed that I knew it and tried to teach me the words to his other favourite samba songs. When I sang him the sex song that Leo taught me, he could not stop laughing, tears streaming down his face. "Ooh, they teach you well in Sorriso. The girls there are nice, but not as nice as São Paulo. You use this on them?"

Our positive spirits dissipated on arrival at Croydon FC. It couldn't have been less Brazilian but Miguel was desperate for this chance. He started the game in a manic state of passion, kicking every ball, chasing everything and tackling aggressively.

Just 10 minutes into the game, he produced a piece of quality, lobbing the keeper from 20 yards to put us 1-0 up. My team-mates went wild. Many of them were in a similar situation to Miguel, and were playing with just as much intensity.

The Brazilians on our team had migrated to England in search of football riches, but had been left as outcasts. There had been the odd success story, but now they were all free agents looking to work their way back into the professional game. We also had a few Eastern Europeans in the team who had first been attracted to England to work. Football was their side project. For them, and indeed the Brazilians, even menial tasks in England paid far better than they did back home.

The difference with the Brazilians was that while they knew that they could return to their homeland and become profes-sionals again, if only lowly paid, that would be admitting defeat. Playing football in Europe had kudos beyond the money and all of their friends and families were immensely proud. If they admitted defeat they would go back to being nobodies.

After Miguel's opener, emotions heightened, though I have to confess I remained indifferent. I did what was needed to win the game but nothing more. Miguel was still racing around like a child on E numbers and just after the half-hour mark his excitement boiled over.

In trying to usher the ball out for a goal-kick, an opposition defender blocked out Miguel perfectly legally. Miguel took exception, however, and proceeded to head-butt him in the chest. The referee didn't see it. Less than a minute later, Miguel went in to a challenge with the opposition left back, overstretch-ing himself and falling awkwardly. He screamed with pain and looked down at his elbow. It was not what an elbow should look like. Bones were at funny angles and a big lump was stick-ing out of his arm.

I don't remember much about the rest of the game but I

do remember the short drive to Croydon A&E and the long wait in the grey building. Anderson was there too – with three Brazilian girls and two men, all in their early 20s. The girls were beautiful. I had spotted them on the sidelines at our game, and now I was trying to get a good look at them without making eye contact. It seemed every other man in the waiting room was doing the same. They knew we were looking, and you could tell that they enjoyed the attention.

About an hour into our wait, the doctor emerged with news that Miguel would be OK. His elbow had dislocated but had been reset. Satisfied, the three girls left to the notable disappointment of every man in the room. Anderson nudged me.

'Hey, Seth. Those three girls – you like?' he asked. I nodded and told him that they were very attractive. Anderson smiled, his eyes twinkling. 'They have to be beautiful. They are prostitutes. See the one in red? If you want to hire her it costs you £500 an hour.'

Eventually Miguel re-emerged with his arm in a sling. Anderson asked if I was hungry. I told him I was and he hatched a plan that involved me driving us all back to the home of the two mystery men who had been with us and who would be cooking as a reward for me giving them a lift. 'Right, we go to St. Albans', Anderson instructed, 'That is where we eat. These two, they live in the house of Denilson. They are his cousins.'

Excitement overcame my hunger. We were going to the home of the Arsenal midfield player and Anderson's client. I had always had a soft spot for Arsenal, not just because of family history but also because of the way Arsene Wenger had them playing, and would be meeting a Brazilian international. But when, after two hours of fighting through London traffic, we got to St. Albans I felt a degree of disappointment. I hadn't expected the house of a Premier League footballer to be so ordinary. Sure, it was in a gated estate, but it wasn't anything special. There wasn't a long gravel drive leading up to a grand door. It was just a normal house.

Denilson opened the front door. He was wearing a plain white T-shirt and grey jogging bottoms. I took great pride that I owned the same outfit. He beckoned us in, high-fiving each of us as we entered. Anderson was singled out for special treatment; he got a hug. Miguel was the last out of the car, and Denilson showed shock at his sling, putting his hand over his mouth and pointing.

I was led in to the kitchen and given a glass of water. One of the cousins turned the oven on and began preparing some rice and beans. Glass of water in hand, I moved into the living room, where Denilson was watching the Sky Sports coverage of Manchester United's game against Newcastle. Rooney had just scored for United, and Denilson was carefully analysing the move. Satisfied, he nodded, admitting that Rooney had made a good goal.

I agreed with him and once he returned to his laptop I began to investigate the room. It was a footballing haven, documenting all of Denilson's successes in the sport. Barclays 'Man of the Match' Champagne bottles stood to attention around the fireplace. There were pictures on the wall of all of the teams that Denilson had played for and match shirts were hung. He was clearly, understandably, proud of where he had come from and what he had achieved.

After several minutes of speaking with friends on his laptop, and then with Anderson, Denilson turned his attention to me. Like Miguel, he couldn't comprehend why an Englishman would want to go to Brazil to play football when he could just stay in England. Still, he asked me all about Sorriso, whether I liked it, and about playing non-League football in England. He seemed pretty interested, despite continuing to message his friends on his laptop while speaking to me.

His paucity of English didn't really help our conversation, however, and I tried to use my broken Brazilian Portuguese, but even though he could barely muster a full sentence, everyone in the room clung to his every word. He just had an aura about him that commanded respect and everyone's full attention. Whenever he made a joke, the whole room burst into laughter, even if it wasn't much good. Manchester United had taken an unassailable lead by the time the rice and beans were ready.

'Hey, you like rice and beans?' Denilson asked as his youngest cousin handed us our plates.

I told him I was sick of them. I'd had them twice a day every day for the whole time I was in Sorriso. Even on Christmas Day.

'How?' he said, looking shocked. 'It is the dish of Brazil. Our skill, our football, our creation. All from this dish. Brazilians are good at football because of our rice and beans.'

One of his cousins, the baby-faced Bolinho – little cake – chipped in. 'Our rice and beans help, Seth. You must have felt better on the pitch after all that food in Sorriso?' he said. 'This is not the only reason that we are so good at football. In Brazil, kids don't have much growing up. They don't have many toys. They don't have all these video games. All they have is a ball. To have fun as a kid you play football. They are not camped up inside. They are outside, on the streets, in the fields, on the courts. all playing football.

'When these kids get to the professional level the training is very good,' Bolinho added. 'At first, a club will not coach a kid. They will give him a ball and say, "go play" and make them play in all positions. They only get given a position when they are 13 or 14 years old. The training is very hard and they work you very hard to become a good player. Playing futsal helps us too. Mainly, though, we just love football. We don't take football just as a profession. It is a passion.'

Everyone was looking at Denilson as he began eating. After a huge mouthful, he made an appreciative 'mmm'. The whole room could relax now. Denilson approved.

The food was indeed pretty good. The beef wasn't nearly as salty as in Casa dos Filtros and the *feijoada* had flavour to it. I was enjoying myself in the company of my Brazilian friends and my mood improved at the suggestion of dessert.

Suddenly Miguel's phone beeped. It was one of the women that Anderson had told me were prostitutes, the one in red. Miguel had first met her at a party thrown at Denilson's house a few weeks before. She had seemingly developed an unhealthy obsession with him and she wanted to see him. Now. That would be the only way that she could check he was OK. She wouldn't take his word that he was all right. She had to see for herself.

Miguel seemed resigned to the fact that he would have to accept this beautiful woman's request and asked if I would take him. I didn't want to leave this other world, this world of fame, fortune and success, but I recognised my commitment to Anderson. Miguel had decided he would go, and Anderson would not let Denilson take him. I was the only other person who could drive him. Anderson would be staying in St Albans that night anyway and Denilson was soon going to bed. I hugged Denilson and his cousins, and then left.

It only took about 30 minutes to get Miguel to the woman's flat on Oxford Street. She was waiting outside for us, eager to have Miguel to herself. She looked even more stunning than earlier. Miguel was a lucky man, and was admittedly delighted at the prospect of 'free sex'. 'Me', he had said with a smile on the drive down, 'man I don't pay'.

Making the most of his injured elbow for her benefit, Miguel gingerly stepped out of the car. She rushed to his side and ushered him in to the building. She quickly returned, and thanked me for driving Miguel. She went into her handbag and produced a crisp £50 note along with a crumpled £20. Seventy pounds! I wasn't sure which I'd boast more to my friends about – meeting Denilson or getting paid £70 by a prostitute. Somehow I felt that the latter would make for the better boast. Life is never dull around Brazilians.

26
DEATH OF A DREAM

The Chairman decided not to renew Mosca's contract at the end of my season in Sorriso. Instead he brought in Capone in a player-manager role. As is usual in Brazil, the majority of the SEC squad left for pastures new and Capone's squad consisted mainly of players he had relocated from São Paulo and even more of his family. He subsequently relegated them to the Mato Grosso second division.

Dudu and Felipe were the only survivors in Capone's squad from our Copa São Paulo team. Rian, apprentice to Trevor, The King of Love, was also supposed to play for Capone, but he fathered a second child and signed for Fluminese's youth team instead. He was only 15. As for The King of Love himself, well, he signed for Katsetsart in Thailand and quickly became the fans' favourite player. Such was his impact that he was soon given the nickname of Tregol. 'Trevor 11' was the most popular shirt in the club shop. At nights Trevor would sit back and sigh contentedly. It was nice not to be booed any more but to be loved, and the training was less strenuous, giving him more energy to satisfy his urges.

The Chairman took most of the blame for SEC's relegation. Of course he sacked Capone immediately, but that was not enough for the fans. They wanted his head too. He had spent most of the season messaging me over the internet and telling me how I was wasting my time going to university. My true calling, he said, was to play football in Brazil. He told me

I could have been a star, offered me 1,000 Reais a month and emphasised how important I'd be to SEC. When I told him I'd return after my degree, he sneered that it would be too late by then, my talent would have disappeared. Still, we stayed close, and he always signed off our conversations with '*abracao irmao*' (a big hug, brother).

The next year he was in trouble. He no longer messaged me telling me that I had to come to Brazil. Instead he asked me for money. He was no longer in Sorriso and had no income. Of course I must have money, he said, I lived in England and everyone is rich there. I told him that I was sorry, but I had no money to give him. He replied that he would come to England and stay in my house. He would become a teacher in a local school – how hard could that be? And while he was on the subject, just how much did a weekly food shop cost?

The Chairman spent about 18 months begging for money over the internet. His beautiful girlfriend was no longer with him. That figured now he was broke and desperate. Then, suddenly, he received a call out of the blue from Palmas Futebol e Regatas Clube in the state of Tocantins. They needed a new director – could he help out?

He perked up and no longer begged me for money. I could still be a star and I was still a fool for turning down his regular contract offers, he said. Once I gave in and told him that yes, go on then, I'd take a contract. Two weeks later there was a problem. Then there wasn't. I was his brother and he loved me more than anything in the world. It was never going to work out again, though.

The Chairman managed to accumulate enough money in Tocantins to fall in love again. His new girlfriend was not as beautiful as his last one, and she was not young enough to pass for his daughter, but the Chairman still loved her deeply. They got engaged and were planning to marry in 2015.

He still speaks to me over the internet and still gently offers me the chance to join him in Brazil every now and then but without the same insistence. He actually uses me more as a motivational speaker nowadays. Every few months I receive a very expensive phone call, just before which the Chairman warns me over the internet that he wants me to speak to his whole team to motivate them. These motivational speeches, over speaker phone, only ever amount to the Chairman calling me a *boiola* and telling me to 'sing Elton John, sing', but they seem to be a great success. Occasionally he passes me on to the team's manager, but we still can't understand each other well enough to make sense of what each of us is saying. I think he wants me to sign for his team.

The Chairman was not the only person to message me. Elias also stayed in touch for a while. He channelled most of his energies into an election campaign to stand as a member of the Sorriso municipal council. He knew lots of people in his municipality already, but this position would allow him to make even more friends. He romped home with a landslide victory, and celebrated with a wild night. Deciding that luck was on his side, he sent me a lengthy poem over the internet declaring his love for me. It read:

I wanted to be Romeo and Juliet in the past,
    An epic dream which brings the beloved baby.
I was drowning in a sea of illusion.
    I am your mermaid.

He'd thoughtfully given me a copy of the poem in both Portuguese and English. I told him that I loved him too, brother. He never replied.

Yago still speaks to me in English. His ability to be Google translate is improving and he is doing a degree in the United States, at Tabor College in Kansas. He dreams of gaining an Italian passport so he can live in Europe. Andrei, too, dreams of Europe.

Leandro was living his dream. After SEC he moved to the Flamengo youth team and from there he signed for Clube Atletico 3 de Febrero of Paraguay, who now play in the Paraguayan second division after relegation. Football allowed him to escape poverty. He still sent money back to his family, who were just as grateful and proud as they had ever been. Every night Leandro thanked God for his good fortune. He even changed his name to Leandro de Jesus.

Aroldo still asks to be called '*negao*'. He still doesn't think it is racist. As with many of my friends, he used his social media profile to be particularly vocal against the Brazilian government. The love for football was immense but there was too an anger at how the government was investing so much money – more than £8 billion – into the World Cup finals of 2014 when there were pressing social issues of poverty and inequality. A move to raise the minimum wage was welcome, helping to lift millions out of extreme poverty, but there was still much to be done. Hospitals, schools and public transport all needed vast improvements but taxes for poor public amenities increased along with the cost of living despite a growing economy.

In football, ticket prices were rising extortionately. The cheapest seats for even a mid-table fixture in the top flight can be 160 Reais – £50 – just 10 Reais fewer than a ticket to a World Cup quarter-final. To gauge how much that is in real terms, it is worth considering that the average Brazilian salary is around a fifth of that in England. As a consequence, the working class and the burgeoning lower-middle class are in danger of being frozen out of the game.

If it is not careful, the game in Brazil will come full circle, returning to Charlie Williams's days and becoming a plaything of the moneyed elite. Much of the burgeoning lower-middle class and working classes are black while few of the upper classes are black. The predominantly white make-up of Brazilian crowds in these new stadiums was reflecting the economic inequality that came with a racial inequality at odds with Brazil's own view that it is a model of racial integration. But it will only have reached that when Aroldo does not ask people to call him *negao*.

I was unable to stay in contact with some of my team-mates. I can only guess as to Leo's fate. There is just as much chance that he has become a superstar as there is that he is in prison. I spoke with Chandler for a few months after getting home but that went quiet. I was never going to be able to keep in contact with Fernando. He didn't have a telephone number, and had no internet access in his favela. Even when we were able to access the internet at Sorriso he refrained, instead deciding to buy an ice lolly and sit in the corner. I guess he never wanted to tease himself with what he knew he couldn't have.

As for me, I took up my place at Loughborough and carried on playing futsal in the FA National League, resulting in a call-up to the England under-21 side, then England B. The skills I had learned in Brazil were put to good use. Everything truly does happen for the best. It was a good time, too, to be playing the sport with England on the up, even if from a low base. In 2014, England were ranked 82nd in the world, one place above Tahiti, but there was growing media interest and coverage for the National League. Brazil are of course number one in the world. As with the World Cup itself, they have won the futsal version five times.

And as with the full game, the Brazilian futsal style is different from any other nation. It is less structured, relying less on team work and more on individual brilliance, and so has given a platform for some of the most brilliant individuals to hone their talents. Neymar, Robinho, Ronaldinho and even Pele all acknowledge the significance of the game. It was, said Pele, 'very, very important, no doubt.'

I continued to receive regular offers from Brazilian clubs, and not just from the Chairman. Despite his refusal to play me in the Copa São Paulo, Emerson tried to get me to sign for three separate teams. Anderson asked me to consider numerous clubs while former directors from Sorriso offered me deals and even journalists tried to sort me out.

I had become a bit of a celebrity, not the sort who might get a call-up for Big Brother Brazil or 'papped' for the South American edition of *Hello!* magazine but it was nice that I had made a bit of a name for myself. I guess the best example was on the bus journey to the Copa São Paulo when we were 11 hours South of Sorriso in the state of Goiana and had stopped for a break. There in a *banheiro* – a washroom – I was recognised by a man who seemed delighted to meet me and warmly shook my hand whilst professing his love of England. Such warmth from Brazilians towards me was touchingly common.

Some time after returning home, there was one moment when I thought that I'd hit the big time. A club official from Fluminese contacted me. He had read about the link between me and Charlie Williams and would be honoured to have me over to Rio so I could trial with the first team. As with all of the offers I received from Brazil in those early days at university, I was ecstatic. I could finally go back to Brazil. I could relive the dream.

But reality would intrude. Most of the Brazilians I encountered had a frustrating inability to organise and see things through. It was a wonder I made it out there in the first place. There would always be complications with any offer I received

– financial issues, contractual issues, visa issues, management issues, accommodation issues, U-turns. I soon learned not to get my hopes up and that proved wise. Nothing ever came of the offers. I did wonder how they were going to host a World Cup.

Then, just as I was finishing my writing of this book, came some news that stunned me and forced me to re-examine much of what I thought about Brazil in general and Sorriso in particular. Elias, I was informed by a journalist with whom I was in contact out there, had been murdered. No wonder there had been no reply to my email saying that 'I love you too, brother.'

I couldn't believe it. I felt numb. How could someone do that to someone so loved? How could someone take away one of Earth's good souls in such a fit of rage? How could anyone dislike someone so loveable, so full of life? And how could someone so full of life have his life taken away?

Elias was 31 years old when he was stabbed 15 times in what the police described as a 'brutal murder' in the early hours of 21st December 2012. The killer, who was believed to be in an intimate relationship with Elias, was seen fleeing naked down the street where Elias lived shortly after the murder. Witnesses reported they had seen Elias, who was also naked, running to his gate screaming for help after being stabbed in his back and neck. As he reached the gate he collapsed.

The police wanted to interview a 22-year-old man who had left his wallet, clothes and documents in Elias's house, but he fled Sorriso and went into hiding. Still almost 18 months on he had not been found. Some who knew him said that he was also in a stable relationship with a 25-year-old woman at the time, and that he kept his relationship with Elias quiet. Others say that Elias and this man's relationship was well known.

Theories grew up around his death beyond it being a dispute between two men. Jacob, a Sorriso supporter whom

I befriended, claimed that some believed that Elias was murdered for political reasons, that he was becoming too powerful politically. Yago didn't believe it. He says that Elias never did anything to hurt anyone and never would, so couldn't believe that someone would ever want to hurt Elias.

The city of Sorriso went into shock. Elias was like a brother to many and known to every single inhabitant. The city had never had such a traumatic experience in its history, according to Yago, and the sense of mourning remains. On 21st December 2013, one year on, they came together to remember him and will come to do so four days before Christmas every year.

When I think back to Elias Maciel, to give him his full name, I remember his infectious smile, boundless energy, kindness of heart and love of life. I remember the T-shirt he used to wear regularly. In English it said: Never miss a chance to dance. It summed up his outlook on life. He loved dancing. He loved anything that made anyone happy. He was the source of many people's happiness, and they were the source of his. He was a symbol of the hope for acceptance and equality.

Recognising his immense contribution to local football, the Sorriso football federation renamed their annual city tournament as the Copa Elias Maciel but any pleasure he might have derived from that knowledge would have been overshadowed by what happened to the club of which he was a director. For Sorriso Esporte Clube was closed down.

SEC did manage to win promotion back from the second division to the top flight of the Campeonato Matogrossense at the first time of asking but it transpired that a few of the directors had been using the club for money laundering. The local government was putting money into the club and grew tired of the losses, the corruption and the politics. That and the fact that it was 20 years since any success, the winning of the state title. The will to keep the club going disappeared. The stadium was given over to American football.

Yago emailed me. 'Sorriso has got so much money, you got no idea. They are the biggest producer of soybean. So much of the world's production of soybean is Sorriso,' he wrote. 'In the past people wanted to put money into the football team. But the money always went missing. People always mysteriously took the money back out of SEC.'

Originally, Sorriso was supposed to grow into a huge city, Yago added. Huge government sums were invested and the football club was supposed to grow alongside. But much money went 'missing' down the years. It explained why SEC were Mato Grosso champions in 1992 and 1993, in the first decade after the city was built, but have won nothing since.

It left the city with a team in debt who couldn't afford quality players. Eventually the rich and powerful people of Sorriso got fed up. As much as they loved having a football team that they supported with such passion, it seems they loved their money even more. People no longer wanted to sponsor SEC. They knew the rumours that money put into the team went missing. They didn't think it was worth the risk.

Elias's death and the folding of the club left me questioning all the good things on and off the football field I had encountered in my formative experience. Was I just a naive kid wanting to believe the best while ignoring all the bad?

I like to think not. I did question what went on around me, in such as attitudes to homosexuality and race, and did seek to understand more about both the world's favourite sport and its role in an astonishingly vibrant culture and nation that could be maddening but also so uplifting.

Above all, I loved its humanity and all its drawbacks and defects only further endeared to me a nation of happy, laid-back people laughing their way through life with a ball at their feet. I use the word people as they always seemed a collective to me. Nobody ever seemed to be left on their own. Everyone was a friend. I often thought back to what Cassius said: London is a cold place, Brazil is a warm place.

Not only did I learn so much from their style of football, I learned to love their style of life. And not a day goes by now when I don't reflect on my time in Brazil and look back with pleasure, despite all that I have subsequently discovered and reflected upon. I learned, laughed and experienced so much and met so many good, happy and joyful people who changed my outlook on life for the better. I stepped out of my comfort zone and made the best investment possible in my future. I was the boy in Brazil who played out his childhood dream, was liberated and learned lessons that eased me into adulthood. Gap years are common among school-leavers these days. Not one like this.

It was hard, in the light of what happened to Elias, to place my faith in the belief I had learned from the country that everything happens for the best but I am sure he would have endorsed two key Brazilian concepts that I would take forward into life: Always be happy and *Voce e do tamanho dos seus sonhos.* You are the size of your dreams.

Actually, I also think Elias believed himself in everything happening for a reason, though that reason may only become apparent later. Such an attitude is invaluable, it seemed to me, in helping you to be happy. And what was the point of not being happy in life? Life is there to be lived, loved and appreciated. It was Elias's credo and if Fernando and Leandro can do it, given their circumstances and having so little, then so can anyone. I smile when thinking about the size of their dreams. They must be enormous.

Part of my growing-up process may have been what I found out after leaving Sorriso, in my introductions to life's tough and cruel realities. I also think that Elias would want me to recall fondly the positive and joyous times that I loved so much there.

I think Elias, too, would want me to remember the translation of Sorriso. Smile.

BRAZIL

MANAUS

FORTALEZA

NATAL

RECIFE

MATO GROSSO

Sinop

Camaçari
Lauro de Freitas

SALVADOR

SORRISO

Lucas do Rio Verde

CUIABA

Cáceres   Rondonópolis

BRASILIA

BELO HORIZONTE

São Carlos

RIO DE JANEIRO

SÃO PAULO

CURITIBA

PORTO ALEGRE

BRAZIL

SOUTH
AMERICA

0   250   500   750   1000

SCALE IN MILES

ACKNOWLEDGEMENTS

Without the commitment and support of my parents I wouldn't be where I am today. I can count the number of my games Dad has missed on one hand, and at each one he gives me advice to be the best I can be. He was just the same with the manuscript. There's always room for improvement, after all.

In fact, the initial manuscript was heavily influenced by my family, and I thank my Gran for helping me to develop my style, as well as my Aunt Sophie for her lengthy research into our family history. I thank, too, my Aunt Marion, for not only proofreading my manuscript, but also for providing continued inspiration with her successful recovery.

Inspiration for the initial manuscript also came from Alex Bellos, author of the excellent *Futebol*, and Gavin Stone of www.lesrosbifs.com. Gavin gave me a platform to write about my experiences, and the subsequent reaction encouraged me to write this book. Dan Brennan and James Young also contributed much to my understanding of Brazil.

I would not have been able to become a professional in Brazil without the coaching I have had. Kit Carson, Kristian Heames, Michael Skubala, Idafe Perez Jimenez, and Charlie Brewster (who coached me on and off from the age of six to 16 and was so good to me) were all fantastic but I have to single out Guy Walton. Guy was the one who first brought me to Stamford, supported my development and pushed me into the first team. He made Anderson Da Silva's vision possible, and of course I must thank Anderson. Along with Guy he is one of the kindest people I have met, someone who genuinely wants what is best for anyone he comes across. I'm glad he has done well in life.

Thanks also go to my publisher, Ian Ridley. It was an honour to work with such an esteemed writer who has had such great success. He has helped me to learn and develop as a writer.

And then there are the people within the narrative. Thanks to my closest friends for keeping me grounded: Josh Alvey, Chris Bill (Bilf), and Marcus Court. Thanks also to Jamie Murtagh, who spent countless hours up the school with me and a football. Dad says he forgives you for the greenhouse.

To my AMVC mates, with whom I enjoy bites and banter, thank you for the incredible support. But my biggest thanks, however, must go to my Brazilian friends who made my experience so enjoyable. I'll never forget you *meu irmaos. Saudades*. And of course, I will never forget you Elias Maciel. I hope this book is a fitting celebration of your memory. Keep on dancing up there, *irmao*.

Seth Burkett
Loughborough, February 2014

AFTERWORD

These have been tough times for young people: youth unemployment at obscene levels, tuition fees and student debt besetting them and the prospect of owning their own flats or houses looking impossible. Getting a start, for even the most talented, can be depressingly difficult. Sometimes they just need some help, just need a break.

Seth Burkett contacted me in December 2013 via my website www.floodlitdreams.com, which I set up partly to help aspiring young writers. He had finished a manuscript about a season he had spent with a club called Sorriso in the central Brazilian state of Mato Grosso as an 18-year-old youth team player then as the only English professional in the country. He was seeking some feedback.

I really had no intention of publishing other people's books at the time. I had set up my own company, Floodlit Dreams Ltd, simply to publish a controversial book with the former Premier League referee, Mark Halsey – *Added Time: Surviving Cancer, Death Threats and the Premier League* – because the original publishers had pulled out of publishing it due to concerns (that never materialised) that it might be subject to legal action.

In reading Seth's manuscript, however, I began to appreciate both a remarkable story and the admirable bravado of youth. Not only had he written charmingly and honestly of a young man's rites of passage in an alien environment, he had also ventured fascinating insights into the maddening joy of the home of football, with all its issues involving such as race, homophobia and poverty. I particularly enjoyed him identifying the obsessions of Brazil as: football, religion and the three S's – sex, samba and soap opera.

It helped, of course, that it was timely and topical as Brazil's World Cup finals approached. With analysis and opinions, Seth sought to capture and explain the significance and wider story of the nation that embraced the game invented by the English and became the best in the world, taking the sport to new levels of beauty and achievement.

It also helped that he discovered on his journey such a remarkable story in his ancestor Charlie Williams, Arsenal's first professional goalkeeper and – astonishingly – first manager of Fluminense in Rio De Janeiro a century earlier. Then there was the unexpected twist in the tail, and the tale, of tragedy in Sorriso.

After meeting with Seth, I decided to publish. This was a young man of initiative, courage and determination who just needed that break. He certainly deserved one. I know how demanding it is producing a manuscript. I admire anyone who can do it. He had done it before his 23rd birthday. I don't think I could have done so at that age, certainly not one anywhere near as accomplished as his.

It has been a pleasure working with Seth to try and help him tell his story in the best possible way, and to see him developing his style and confidence. I hope you deem this as enjoyable, engaging, poignant and informative a piece of work as I did.

Ian Ridley
St Albans, March 2014

ALSO BY IAN RIDLEY

ALSO BY FLOODLIT DREAMS

Added Time: Surviving Cancer, Death Threats
and the Premier League – with Mark Halsey

Added Time takes you where no other book has gone –
inside the dressing rooms on match days, into the intense
tunnel and on-field conversations and confrontations between
officials and the game's participants. It chronicles the highs
and lows, joy and pain, and reveals the human face of that
man in the middle.

Mark Halsey lifts the lid on surviving the internal politics,
personalities and intrigue of refereeing, on altercations with
Sir Alex Ferguson and earfuls from Wayne Rooney.

Running through Halsey's powerful and poignant story is
his gutsy battle with throat cancer, through surgery and
gruelling treatment, after which the popular Halsey returned
to the top. It granted him no immunity from the dangerous
stresses that can afflict the modern referee, however – stresses
that included those death threats.

What kept him going for 17 years at the top? Strength of
character, a loving family – and the unlikely friendship with
José Mourinho.

**Nominated for Best Biography/Autobiography,
British Sports Book Awards 2014**

'Mark Halsey has been one of our finest referees and has an
inspirational story that goes beyond football'
David Moyes, Manchester United manager, on *Added Time*

ABOUT THE AUTHORS

Seth Burkett is completing an MA in American Literature at Loughborough University after graduating with a degree in Sports Science and English. He is also an England futsal international. *The Boy in Brazil* is his first solo book, written at the age of just 23, after co-writing *The Year of the Hobby* with his Grandmother, Molly Burkett.

Ian Ridley is the author of 10 football books, including the No.1 best-selling *Addicted* with the former Arsenal and England captain, Tony Adams, which was nominated for the William Hill Sports Book of the Year. Three of his other books have also been listed in the British Sports Books Awards. Over a 35-year career, he has written on the game for newspapers including *The Guardian*, *The Daily Telegraph*, *The Independent on Sunday*, *The Observer* and *The Mail on Sunday*, for whom he was Chief Football Writer. He was named Sports Journalist of the Year in the British Press Awards for 2007 and has been nominated on two other occasions.

Photograph by Alex Ridley